The Graves County Boys

THE
GRAVES
COUNTY
BOYS

A Tale of Kentucky Basketball, Perseverance, and the Unlikely Championship of the Cuba Cubs

MARIANNE WALKER
FOREWORD BY JOE B. HALL

UNIVERSITY PRESS OF KENTUCKY

Published by The University Press of Kentucky

Scholarly publisher for the Commonwealth,
serving Bellarmine University, Berea College, Centre College of Kentucky,
Eastern Kentucky University, The Filson Historical Society, Georgetown
College, Kentucky Historical Society, Kentucky State University, Morehead
State University, Murray State University, Northern Kentucky University,
Transylvania University, University of Kentucky, University of Louisville,
and Western Kentucky University.
All rights reserved.

Editorial and Sales Offices: The University Press of Kentucky
663 South Limestone Street, Lexington, Kentucky 40508-4008
www.kentuckypress.com

Library of Congress Cataloging-in-Publication Data

Walker, Marianne, 1933-
  The Graves County boys : a tale of Kentucky basketball, perseverance, and the un-
likely championship of the Cuba Cubs / Marianne Walker ; foreword by Joe B. Hall.
      pages cm
  Includes bibliographical references and index.
  Previously titled: When Cuba conquered Kentucky, 1999.
  Originally published: Nashville, TN : Rutledge Hill Press, 1999.
  ISBN 978-0-8131-4305-7 (pbk. : alk. paper) — ISBN 978-0-8131-4418-4 (epub) —
  ISBN 978-0-8131-4419-1 (pdf)
  1. Cuba Cubs (Basketball team)—History. 2. Basketball—Kentucky—History.
3. School sports—Kentucky—History. I. Title.
  GV885.42.C83W34 2013
  796.323'630976993—dc23   2013023503

This book is printed on acid-free paper meeting the requirements of the
American National Standard for Permanence in Paper for Printed Library
Materials.

Manufactured in the United States of America.

Member of the Association of University Presses

For Ulvester Walker
and in memory of my parents,
Joseph D. and Rose Spatafora-Cascio

Always bear in mind that your own resolution to succeed is more important than any other thing.

—Abraham Lincoln, November 8, 1856,
in a letter to Isham Reavis,
an aspiring law student

Contents

Foreword

The Graves County Boys is a great story from start to finish. It is about a small group of teenagers coming of age in a remote region of Kentucky, where values were passed down from one generation to another. Marianne Walker tells the boys' story so engagingly that this book will appeal to a wide range of readers: of all ages, and whether they are fans of basketball or not. It is a true story about life during the 1940s and early 1950s and about the achievement of dreams. These boys, called the Cuba Cubs, were taught by their young coach, Jack Story, how to make the best use of their individual athletic strengths. Even more important, the coach convinced them they could do something great, something that had never been done before in their area. He taught them not only to dream about success, but how to make their dream come true.

I got caught up in reading this book not only because I love basketball and coached the sport for many years, but also because I have long been interested in this Cuba Cubs team. When the Cubs won the state basketball championship in 1952, I was working and could not get away to see the tournament games. But I had heard how exciting the Cubs were that year and how the team, from the tiny community of Cuba, Kentucky, had captured the hearts of basketball fans from all over.

After I was hired by the University of Kentucky as an assistant to Coach Adolph Rupp and moved back to Lexington in 1965, one of the first things I did was go to the university archives and check out the film of the Cuba Cubs championship game. Having joined the Harlem Globetrotters in 1951 for a European tour, I was intrigued by the way the Cubs imitated the style of some of the Globetrotters. I thought it was great that those kids could perform many of the Trotters' feats so astonishingly well.

However, it was not until I read this book that I had a full appreciation of the extent of what they did. Marianne does not merely describe their games, she also delves into their childhoods and traces the development of their lives, spent in an isolated rural region where indoor plumbing and electricity were not available in all of their homes as late as 1952.

I appreciate what those boys did so much more after reading Marianne's in-depth study of their lives and hardships. Marianne describes the place where the Cubs were born and raised; she tells about their parents and their struggles to eke out a living during the Depression in the 1930s. She also describes their neighbors, the coach, and the school with such immediacy that I felt as if I knew them all and was right there in Graves County with them. She shows how the school, in those days, was the center of community life and how the entire community supported the school and its basketball team.

This book is a lesson in life. It highlights the importance of dedication and determination, both of which require hours and hours of hard work in order to master certain techniques and to develop individual strengths. From all that effort the Cubs made came a confidence that was built on solid ground.

This book is so much more than a story of a basketball season. It is about a dream that some boys and a coach made real for themselves and for an entire community.

The Graves County Boys is so well written that you will find yourself enjoying the entire trip, not just the tournament games. This story is compelling from the first bounce of the ball to the lifting of the trophy.

Coach Joe B. Hall

Preface

The idea for this book came from my friend Pam Thomas who, years ago, suggested I write an article about her husband's high school basketball team. Puzzled, I shook my head no, reminding her that I did not do sports. At that time, Pam was married to Howard Crittenden, who was principal of the large high school in Henderson, Kentucky, where I live. She explained that he had been a star player on his high school team, the Cuba Cubs, in Cuba, Kentucky. His team lost the state championship as juniors but won as seniors in 1952. The players were so good, she boasted, at imitating the Harlem Globetrotters that they drew large crowds to all their games and the manager of the Trotters invited them to St. Louis to attend one of their games in 1951. She wanted me to talk to Howard and some of his teammates, saying she thought I would find some good material to write about.

I was doubtful. Happily immersed in research for a biography I was writing of Margaret Mitchell, author of *Gone With the Wind*, and her Kentucky husband, John Marsh, I was not interested in a basketball story. Only as a courtesy to Pam did I listen to her husband talk about his experiences one evening. We met again later when his childhood friend, the other star player on the team, Charles Floyd, nicknamed Doodle, came from Knoxville, Tennessee, to visit him and Pam. But the more they talked about games, strategies, opponents, and their coach, the more convinced I was that this topic was not for me.

I began to change my mind on the summer day my husband and I went with Howard and Doodle to Graves County, Kentucky, to visit their "hometowns" of Cuba and Pilot Oak. Actually, neither of these places was ever a town; they were tiny farming communities with a few houses, a store, a school, a blacksmith, and a couple of churches. Both are far less populated now than they were when Howard and Doodle were growing up. In those days they were thriving communities. Now they are mostly wide fields and forests. Howard and Doodle gave us a tour of all the locations that were significant in their childhoods. We saw where their homes had once stood in the woods at the end of dirt roads, where their tobacco patches and pastures had been, the locations of their schoolhouse and the pounded-dirt half-court in front of the Pilot Oak Store where they first learned to play basketball. They talked about how their friendship began when they were young children and how much Coach Jack Story had done for them.

In Mayfield, the county seat of Graves County, they introduced us to Donald Poyner, assistant superintendent of Graves County Schools and valedictorian of their class. Donald became a great friend and an enormous help in securing information and guiding me to sources.

My husband and I continued to visit Graves County now and then, collecting bits of information on each trip. Eventually, I met all the other members of the team and learned about their backgrounds. After I had seen all the places so important in the Cubs' childhood and had talked with people who had lived in that same area for years, knew the coach well, and had watched the Cubs grow up, I began to see a way that I could write a story about basketball. But it would be the kind that I would like to read; it would be more about the people who played the game. The fact that I did not know much about basketball turned out to be an advantage to me as a writer, for it enabled me to see the Cubs' story from a different perspective. It was that perspective that intrigued me. To those who wonder if I were intimidated or handicapped by not knowing the sport, I answer no, for I had a championship team, some of them coaches, ready and willing to explain the subject at any and all times.

The result of my first research efforts was a feature article entitled "When Cuba Conquered Kentucky" in the February 26, 1989, edition of the *Louisville Courier-Journal Magazine.* David McGinty, editor of the magazine, and his staff invented that clever but curious title. Readers' response to that article was so remarkable that I decided at some later point I would go back to the Cubs and listen to them finish telling me their whole story. Meanwhile, Rutledge Hill Press in Nashville wanted to publish an expanded version of the magazine article and did so in 1999 when it released a slim volume, borrowing the *Courier-Journal*'s title *When Cuba Conquered Kentucky.* That edition was incomplete and hurried to press, and I was never satisfied with it. I am grateful to have this second edition.

This new edition has a foreword by Coach Joe B. Hall, head basketball coach at the University of Kentucky from 1972 to 1985. He led the Wildcats to their fifth NCAA Championship in 1978 and is the recipient of many honors and awards, including induction into the National Collegiate Basketball Hall of Fame in 2012.

In addition to rewriting some of the chapters and adding more information about the tournaments and about African American teams, I have added some new photos and an updated epilogue. This edition also has an online guide that will be available for coaches and teachers to use in their classrooms. The guide contains suggested discussion and writing topics involving such subjects as basketball rule changes, sportsmanship, character analysis, school discipline, advantages and disadvantages of attending small rural schools, the effects poverty has on children and their families, the role geography plays in shaping the character of the people in a given area, and the importance of setting goals and working to achieve them.

Note on Sources

This book was not easy to research or to write, but work on it was interesting and challenging. For the information I needed this time, I could not do what I had done for other projects—turn to books and papers, all organized nicely in folders in special collection libraries. With the exception of some newspaper articles and a few photographs that I found in the sports library at Eastern Kentucky University in Richmond and in the McCracken County Library in Paducah, I had to find people who had lived in Graves County during the first half of the twentieth century.

Then, after I had found some of these people, I had to earn their confidence before they would answer my questions in depth. This, in turn, required numerous trips to Graves County, Lexington, and Louisville, and countless numbers of telephone calls, letters, and, more recently, e-mails. More often than not, answers just led to more questions, and more searches. Information came in slowly, in bits and pieces, often tangled up in long, rambling narratives about irrelevant subjects.

At first I tape-recorded interviews but soon learned that people were more relaxed and informative when the tape recorder was off. I started taking notes instead. I created a questionnaire of seventeen questions that I mailed to everyone who had been on the Cuba Cubs team or connected with it. I followed up with telephone calls and more visits.

Whenever my task seemed impossible, I remembered Coach Jack Story's golden rule (which I had copied onto a Post-it note and stuck to the top of my computer): "Never give up. The only time you lose is when you quit."

This book, then, is a compilation of oral histories. Information about basketball, the tournaments, daily life, experiences with Coach Story, and all the biographical information about the individual team members came directly from the players themselves: Howard "Howie" Crittenden, Charles "Doodle" Floyd, Joe Buddy Warren, Jimmie Webb, Jimmy Jones, Ted Bradley, and Bill Pollock. These men shared intimate details of their childhood and teenage experiences, both good and bad. Their accounts were vivid and corroborated; one man's version of their shared experiences was not different from another's. I spoke with the major players individually and often—their memories did not ever conflict. They furnished the intimate details that enabled me to write about their lives as I have. I've tried to tell their stories in their own distinctive and interesting voices. In describing some conversations and interactions, I have felt confident in placing myself right there in their past, using direct quotation marks.

They brought Coach Story alive as perhaps no one else could have. So important was the way they explained how Coach Story interacted with them—the distance he always kept between them. He was always in charge. They told me things that only they would know about him, such as how he rarely complimented them and how they craved his praise and approval; how he liked to sit straddling a chair with his big arms on the back of it; how he scowled when he was angry; and how he lowered his voice when he wanted to get their attention.

Coach Story died years before I began my research, but his widow, Mary Lee, was hospitable and helpful. She was only a high school senior when she married Jack, a young teacher at her school. Like me, she was not a sports enthusiast but said she learned early on to accept basketball as the third partner in her marriage because basketball was her husband's passion. My visits with her were all in her home, the one she and Jack moved into after their three children—Rex, Carolyn, and Barbara—were grown and married. While we sat on her sofa and leafed through the scrapbooks she had kept over many years, she reminisced. She told me about their daily life, about her husband's mannerisms and habits, about their work at the school, the teachers, the players, and the cheerleaders, and the troubles he sometimes encountered with them all. She recalled events and people vividly, and I have described them just as she described them to me.

Another major source of my information was Lon Carter Barton, a historian of western Kentucky and an authority on the Jackson Purchase. Lon had a great understanding of the Purchase and its people. As a member of Kentucky's House of Representatives from 1958–1966, he acquired a keen understanding of state government politics. When I first met him, he was a retired history teacher, a bachelor, living in Mayfield in his family's large antebellum home, where he had history books in every room. He joked about his basement, saying it was a landfill of more newspapers and books. After each visit with him, I always left feeling as if I had learned a semester's worth of western Kentucky history and how life was lived in the first half of the twentieth century. My account of the history of the Jackson Purchase and its people is the result of my talks with him.

My description of Little Cubie, later called Cuba, came from several sources: people whose families had lived there for generations, people who were born and reared there in the 1920s, 1930s, and 1940s, and who lived there their entire lives. Much of my information came from Beth Page Belote and her older sister, Hattie Page Glenn, both wonderfully intelligent, educated, and charming women. Beth lived in Mayfield and Hattie, a widow, lived in Louisville, where her husband, Pap Glenn, had been a popular well-known high school coach and later athletic director at Louisville Male High School.

These sisters were the daughters of Marion Page, the physician who lived and raised his family in Cuba and practiced medicine there. They permitted me to read letters their father wrote to his family while he was in the armed services during World War I. They also showed me a journal he kept for a brief time. The few notes he had scribbled about his daily encounters with patients were fascinating and provided a unique insight into the lives of some of the local citizens. That little diary left me wishing he had continued to write in it.

Beth introduced us to La Rue Page, her widowed sister-in-law, who met us one afternoon on the lawn of their family home to show us Dr. Page's office. A small, white-framed, three-room house, it was sturdily built just a few steps away from the main house. I was so happy to see this place, for it was a tangible connection to the past I was most interested in. Everyone I met in Cuba had told me a story about Dr. Page; he had influenced so many lives. Alone in his office, I felt as if I had stepped back into the 1930s. In my mind's eye, I could see the tall, jovial physician, teasing Cornelius Sissons, ancient and arthritic: "Cornelius, you old coot, you don't have a damn bit more business being out of the ground than a mole does."

I enjoyed listening to Pauline Harper, the owner of one of the two general stores in Cuba. She described the times, the stock in her store, the old men called the "store setters," her customers and the routine of their daily lives. She knew Coach Story, his wife, and children well. She also knew all of the boys on the team. One of the Cubs' cheerleaders and classmates, Barbara, her daughter, contributed information about the life of teenagers in the 1940s and early 1950s.

Memorable, too, were visits with the old farmer Otis McPherson and his wife, Roselle. A wonderful couple, they taught me much about how farm life was lived in the past: how tobacco was raised, cured, and sold; how dairy cows were taken care of; how mules were trained, used, and traded. One afternoon Roselle served my husband and me some of her delicious coconut cake with thick white icing sprinkled with toasted coconut; it was the best cake we have ever eaten. The McPhersons' house, shaded by large old trees, and their farm were beautiful, so organized and amazingly immaculate. That old Scotsman kept his tractors, tools, trucks, and car spotless. I am sure his barn was more sanitized than some kitchens.

Although this book is about an all-white high school basketball team from an impoverished rural school in the late 1940s and early 1950s, black high school basketball teams, some from even more impoverished schools, existed then as well. During this period of segregation, blacks and whites could not attend the same schools, and blacks were forbidden to compete in white athletic contests. Although it is likely that some games between the races were played, we have no record of them. Black players had their own state basketball tournaments. To learn about them, I met with Louis Stout, author of *Shadows of the Past: A History of the Kentucky High School Athletic Association*. His book is a valuable source of information and contains a remarkable collection of rare photographs. My discussion of African American high school basketball teams was taken from Stout's book.

Finally, I thank each person named in this book and hope readers enjoy learning about them as much as I did.

The Cuba Cubs, 1951–1952. (Cuba School yearbook photo.)

1

The Cuba Cubs

Sports serve society by providing vivid examples of excellence.
—George F. Will

One rainy afternoon in the fall of 1948, in an old rural Kentucky schoolhouse, Coach Jack Story took his eighth-grade basketball prodigies into the auditorium. He had set up a film projector, a screen, and some folding chairs there. As the boys sat down, he straddled a straight-back wooden chair, folding his thick arms on its back. He talked to them for a few minutes about what it means to be on a basketball team, and then he leaned forward a bit and told them in a low voice the two secrets to playing the game well: "First, you have to learn to move with the ball the way you move without the ball. And second, you have to learn to deceive your opponent. You have to fool him. You have to make him expect anything except what you are really going to do." Then he added, "Now watch this film, and you will see what I am talking about."

He turned out the lights and started the projector, which summoned flickering images of the Harlem Globetrotters. As the film began rolling, the boys were startled. Their eyes widened as they scooted to the edges of their chairs, astonished by what they saw— agile black men shooting, dribbling, and handling the basketball like magicians. They were performing marvelously difficult and quick tricks with the ball and making improbably goofy but amazing shots. They were thrilling to watch, and the boys laughed loudly.

In that darkened room in that old schoolhouse that day, a handful of farm boys went wild with joy. When the film was over, they begged to see it again, and the coach obliged. That film was a revelation to them. The only basketball they had ever seen was played in orthodox games by teams from other rural schools in their own area. This Harlem Globetrotters' game was like nothing they had ever even imagined. The Globetrotters played in a creative, embellished way and with great ease. They looked as if they were having fun doing it, too.

After the boys watched the film for the third time, they begged to see it once more, but Coach Story said no. He told them to get on the court and see if they could do any of the things they had seen the Globetrotters doing. Chattering excitedly, the boys jumped off the stage, grabbed basketballs, and ran onto the floor. Now they had a vision to go along with their experience.

Tossing a ball back and forth between them, two of the youngsters—Doodle and Howie—darted around each other, feinting and laughing. Trying to perform some of the Globetrotters' feats just came naturally to those two. Immediately, Doodle began trying to imitate Globetrotter Reece "Goose" Tatum, famous for both his leaping ability and his clowning. Howie, who was already showing promise of being an exceptional ball handler, chose to imitate Marques Haynes, said to be the most spectacular dribbler in basketball history.

Coach Story had an uncanny ability to spot raw athletic talent, and he saw it in these five boys. He showed them this film after he had watched them several times playing on the school grounds. Instinctively, he knew that they had the potential he had been looking for. Moreover, he loved their boyish, comic ball-handling antics and knew they would be thrilled seeing the Globetrotters film. They would learn from it, too. His varsity players would not; they would not have reacted to the film the way these eighth graders did, nor were they in love with basketball the ways these little guys were. Coach Story did not show the film or even discuss the Globetrotters with the varsity team.

Weeks earlier, he had explained to the younger boys how a team gets to compete in a state tournament and what an honor it is to win the championship, especially for a small school like theirs. Their school had never sent a team to the state tournament. He was convinced, he said, as he looked them in the eye, that they had the ability to win the state championship. He asked them to keep thinking about what an honor it would be to win that trophy. "It means you have whipped the best teams in the whole state," he exclaimed. "It means *you* at that moment in time are the best!" The boys left that afternoon sold on the idea that, yes, they were going to do it. They would win the championship trophy their senior year. The next afternoon, while he was daydreaming in study hall, Jimmie Webb, the boy with curly dark hair, took out his barlow knife and carved the words *Cuba Cubs State Champions 1952* on the underside of his old desk table.

That same day Jack Story showed the film and saw the boys' reaction to it, he decided to train them to become a *championship* team. The one problem he anticipated, though, was their tendency to be rowdy, undisciplined. He knew that they might possibly require a little corporal punishment at times. As not only the coach but also the principal of the Cuba School, he often had to deal with unruly students. Adhering to the standards of his day, he kept a heavy wooden paddle hidden in his office. Although he seldom used it, he

Jack Story in 1940. (Photo courtesy of Barbara Story Crowell.)

never hesitated to do so when he deemed it necessary. He picked up his paddle and walked into the gym, where he stood silently studying the boys with his arms folded across his chest, the paddle—in plain view—in his right hand.

After watching the Harlem Globetrotters play, the boys were exuberant. They did not notice the coach or his paddle. The stage, which was a platform about three and a half feet high built at one end of the gymnasium, was so close to the basketball court that balls often bounced onto it, as one did that afternoon. Coach Story watched as Joe Buddy Warren jumped onto the stage to retrieve the ball. Instead of running directly back to the court, he jumped off the stage and casually strolled along beside it, talking and giggling as he bounced the ball along the top edge of the stage.

The boys froze when they heard Coach Story shout, "Stop!" and saw him walking briskly toward them. As he got closer, he said to Joe Buddy, "Just what do you think you are doing, son? Do you think that they are going to let you bounce a ball on anything except the court in a game?" Scanning the somber group with a mean stare, he said he thought that they wanted to become a championship team. Well, if that were the case, he scolded, they had better start paying attention to what they did with that basketball. They'd better learn those fundamentals and practice them every day. Then came his warning: "Don't you ever let me catch any one of you doing anything with a basketball that you cannot do in a game. If you cannot use it in a game, then do not do it! Do you understand that?" He looked each one of them in the eye and then all of a sudden he swung that paddle, popping Joe Buddy's seat hard as he muttered, "And may this help you to remember."

This incident would be the first of many times during the next four years that the boys made Jack Story angry. But on that particular day those boys had the hardest time trying to conceal their laughter at Coach Story's angry face and Joe Buddy's grim red one.

2

The Little Crossroads Team

Nothing is achieved before it is thoroughly attempted.
—Sir Philip Sidney

With their diligent daily practice and with the guidance of their coach, the Cubs—by the time they were juniors—had quite a wonderful reputation in western Kentucky and West Tennessee. Known as the Cuba Cubs from little Cuba, Kentucky, they were a popular and respected team, well grounded in the fundamentals. They played uniquely, with a flair that resembled the Harlem Globetrotters, and everywhere they played, the gyms were packed with spectators. As juniors, they had already earned their right to compete in the state tournament to be held in Memorial Coliseum in Lexington, Kentucky, in mid-March 1951.

Two days before the coach and the team left for Lexington in 1951 to compete in the state tournament, Jack Story had a telephone interview with Edd Kellow, sportswriter for the *Paducah Sun-Democrat*. He talked about his team's successful record for the season (33-2), noting that in thirty-five ball games, the Cubs had hit an amazing 45 percent of their shots from the field and 68 percent from the free-throw line. He added that he and the boys planned to keep that pace up in Lexington. Then he stammered, "You can't believe it—you won't believe it—this place has gone state tournament crazy. And I want you to see for yourself. I believe that everyone from Cuba is going to Lexington. And from the number of requests for tickets, I'm not sure that all Graves and Fulton counties aren't going to be there with us."

The old school buses were in no shape to make the long trip, so everyone who had a car or truck offered to take someone who had no ride. Getting ready for the trip was a joyful communal effort. By 4:00 that blustery, cold, dark Wednesday morning of March 14, 1951, all of Graves County was awake and hurrying about. In Mayfield, Pilot Oak, and Cuba, trucks and cars were already parked outside of the stores where people were to meet to share rides. Cuba supporters from all the little neighboring places, including Lynnville, Water Valley, Sedalia, Dukedom, and Fulton, gathered at their stores and schools to form their own caravans and car pools.

In other parts of western Kentucky similar car pools were organized. It was a merry pilgrimage starting out early that morning. At one point, the heavy traffic on Highway 31W headed east made it look as if all of western Kentucky were being evacuated.

Graves County alone accounted for forty automobiles making up the long motorcade to Lexington. The story the newspapers put out was that everybody in Cuba went to the state tournament except Harry McClain. He stayed home because he had agreed to milk everybody's cows and to do so had rigged up a mechanical milking device on his pickup truck. Harry did stay to look after things for others, but he was not the only person who remained. Aside from those too old or ill to go were Doodle's, Howie's, and Jimmie Webb's parents. They had not attended any of their sons' games, even the ones played in Cuba. Perhaps it was not just their lack of interest this time, but also their lack of money to travel that kept them at home.

Jack Story never placed any value on cheerleaders, as important as they were to the school and to the team. To him, those girls were a nuisance, a major distraction for the players. He never even assigned a faculty advisor to them, so they managed their own little organization. He made no arrangements for them to go to the tournament, so they rode with their families or friends and made their own hotel reservations. Yet he had to approve all their routines. Just before the trip to Lexington, he had condemned their latest cheer when he found them practicing this little hip-grinding, hand-waving strutting dance while they chanted: *Roosters chew tobacco. Hens dip snuff. Come on Cuba, strut your stuff! Strut! Strut! Strut! Come on, Cuba, strut your stuff!*

Those in Graves County who did not own a radio frantically tried to buy one once they learned that Cuba had won the regional tournament by beating the formidable Paducah Tilghman 61-46. In fact, all the stores in Mayfield and in Fulton sold out of radios in a flash once the word was out that Coach Story was taking his team to the state tournament.

The day the tournament began, it was not business as usual in the county. The few people in Pilot Oak who had not gone to Lexington went to Fred Wagoner's store to listen to the games on the radio there. In Cuba, they went to Carl Rhodes's store. In these small communities, where people generally had no way to distinguish themselves as excellent in any area, the success of "their" boys brought distinction to them. They were hopeful, happy, and proud of Coach Story and his team.

Over the three days before the Cubs' departure, fans in Cuba and Pilot Oak held celebrations of all kinds—luncheons, pep rallies, informal get-togethers, and a banquet the night before their departure. Nearly every person in the area had contributed to the

Cubs' effort in some way, so each individual felt as if he or she had a stake in the Cubs' success. The farmers had scraped together enough money to buy the boys new warm-up suits, socks, and underwear. Aught McClain, father of one of the Cubs' classmates and a barber, gave free haircuts to Coach Story and to each of the Cubs. Mary Lee Story, Coach Story's wife, bought the players new satiny gold and green uniforms and shoes with earnings she had saved from the concession and supply stand she ran at the school. Some men who had jobs in Mayfield collected enough money to buy basketballs, which Coach Story painted green and gold—the school colors.

The owners of the four men's clothing stores in Mayfield gave the coach and each player a complete suit of clothes, including two white shirts, ties, socks, dress shoes, topcoats, and more underwear. Other merchants collected money to pay for the team's travel expenses, hotel rooms, and meals. They even gave each boy a crisp new $20 bill, an extravagant amount of spending money. Everything the community could do had been done for them, and now the rest was up to the Cubs and the coach.

The drive to Lexington was about 280 miles and took the better part of a day. They traveled on two-lane roads winding through one small town after another. The highway speed limit was fifty or fifty-five miles an hour, and having to stop in every town and hamlet for stoplights, stop signs, intersections, and railroad crossings made the ride even slower.

Some of the team's starters—Howie Crittenden, Charles "Doodle" Floyd, Joe Buddy Warren, Raymon McClure, and Jimmie Webb or Jimmy Jones—rode with Coach Story and his wife. On previous trips they had crowded into Coach's secondhand Plymouth, but this time they all rode in his spacious new Kaiser. He was so happy to be taking his team to the state tournament that he splurged on a new automobile, without saying anything to his wife beforehand. The morning after winning the regional tournament, he drove to Paducah, a city about twenty-four miles from Mayfield, where he lived, and paid over $3,000 plus the trade-in value of his Plymouth for this beautiful Kaiser. Jack Story felt proud and confident driving his new four-door, two-toned, grass green sedan with its golden-tan interior—colors that matched the Cuba School colors.

Nearly all cars then were built big, but this Kaiser was really big. Unlike the Plymouth, it had ample room for three adults to sit in the front and four in the back, comfortably. The manufacturers had completely redesigned the Kaiser that year, making it less boxy, giving it more glass, more head- and legroom. It was advertised as "the new Anatomic Design, made to fit the human anatomy." In addition to its color, that selling pitch may have been the very thing that attracted Jack Story to this car. At six feet three and 260 or more pounds, he needed a large car to drive himself, his wife, and five slender but long-legged basketball players around the state.

This car was classy looking, too. Its huge windshield header sloped down on each side and had a V in the middle, giving it the seagull wing appearance that became Kaiser's trademark. With its shiny K-and-buffalo badge and a dartlike mascot sitting in the center of the hood, this automobile was the grandest thing that Coach Story and the Cubs had ever seen on the highway, and riding in it made them feel like world-class winners.

They arrived in Lexington early afternoon that cold, crisp day. Coach Story parked near the front of Memorial Coliseum. Before getting out of his car, he and the others sat silently, staring out the window at the new building for a minute or so.

Just one year earlier, the large arena had been added to the campus of the University of Kentucky as a memorial to Kentuckians who had died in the two world wars. With its capacity to seat 12,500, it was said to be the largest arena in the South. That next day, for the first time, it was to be the site of the Kentucky Boys' Sweet Sixteen High School Basketball Tournament.

Breaking the silence, Mary Lee, seated next to Coach Story, spoke first: "Well, why are we sitting here? Let's all go look inside."

The wide doors of the Kaiser popped open and five teenage boys, the coach, and his wife climbed out. While the boys ran ahead to the entrance of the Coliseum, Jack and Mary Lee stood waiting on the sidewalk for the other cars with players and team managers to arrive. Dressed in his good-luck brown suit, the same color Coach Adolph Rupp always wore to games, and a brown felt hat cocked to one side of his head, Jack Story leaned back, stretching slightly, pressing his hands into his lower back as if to ease an old pain. He smiled as he watched his starters entering the building that they had dreamed of seeing.

Inside the Coliseum, the boys stood in awe, struck by the wonder of newness and the stillness that pervades a battlefield before a battle. Staring at the ceiling, Jimmie Webb whispered, "This is the first place I've ever been in where I couldn't throw the ball and hit the ceiling." The others turned to look at him and then looked up silently.

Accustomed to playing on creaky wooden gym floors in rural schools, Howie knelt down and ran his hand over the smooth hardwood, saying, "This looks and feels just like polished glass!" Pointing his finger up and down at the floor, Joe Buddy merrily exclaimed, "Yeah! And just think. We are going to play on *this* floor. This is the floor the Kentucky Wildcats play on! And they already have won two NCAAs. And I bet they win it again this year. Holy cow! I can't believe we're here!"

They laughed. This was the first time they had been so far out in the world, and they had mixed feelings of fear, wonder, and excitement. This was the place and the moment they had been dreaming about and working toward since they were in the eighth grade, and here they were as juniors—a year earlier than planned.

Their trip that day was long in more than one way. They had

ridden from their tiny rural community of Cuba, Kentucky, to Lexington, the second largest city in the Commonwealth and the home of the winningest college basketball team in the nation—the University of Kentucky Wildcats—and the winningest coach—Adolph Rupp.

After their brief stop at the Coliseum, Coach Story drove the boys to the Phoenix Hotel where they and their supporters were staying. On their way, they listened to a sports broadcaster on the car radio talk about the teams playing in the tournament the next day. As he described them as the unknowns, the little crossroads team, they tensed up, listening to him say such things as "We don't know what to expect from the Cuba Cubs from way down yonder in Graves County. That's in the Jackson Purchase region and is about as far west as you can go and still be in Kentucky. They are the mysterious underdogs in this tourney. Their whole school has only about a hundred students." Although some of the other smaller schools in western Kentucky were known throughout the state, he said Cuba was not one of them. He named the familiar larger high schools—Paducah Tilghman and Owensboro Senior High—saying how well respected they were.

He listed the achievements of Covington Holmes, winner of the Ninth Region, whom the Cubs would face that next evening. He pointed out that the Holmes team, from a large high school in Covington, a city directly across the Ohio River from Cincinnati, was one of the tallest aggregations in the state and one of the most powerful teams, one not easily defeated. Doodle winced when he heard him add, "The tallest player on Cuba's team is six feet four, so rebounding might be a problem for them."

Thus, the first thing the Cubs heard upon arriving in Lexington was this broadcaster's view that they were not expected to survive their first battle in the tournament. The boys sighed. The coach turned off the radio.

3

The Clutch

It is not enough to fight. It is the spirit which we bring to the fight
that decides the issue. It is morale that wins the victory.
—George C. Marshall

The next evening, Thursday, March 15, 1951, in the locker room
just before the first game was to begin, Coach Story went over their
plan. Although he had never seen Covington Holmes, their opponent, play before, he gave his boys what knowledge he had about
how he thought they would play, who their best players were, and
what the Cubs should do to prevent them from scoring. In his usual
calm manner, he told them that although the other team members
were taller than they were, not to let their opponents fake them.
He assured them that they could control the rebounds and block
Holmes out, that they were better than Holmes. Then he went over
the basic steps that he had taught them when they were eighth graders, steps that he had had them practice regularly since then, steps
that they could recite easily: (1) You get in front of your man, push
your butt against him so he cannot get around you; (2) As you jump

to get the ball, make yourself bigger by spreading your legs wide and raising your elbows up and out; (3) Hold onto the ball so your opponent cannot slap it out of your hands; (4) If your elbows are spread out and raised, your opponent will not be able to touch the ball.

Sharing their nervousness but appearing at ease, Coach Story stood up and looked directly into their young faces so filled with emotion. He reminded them that they had beaten taller players before and that they could beat these guys. And then, as always when facing a strong opponent, he repeated his warning, "Remember, when you go out there, do not look at them! It makes you look like you're dreading them."

Just as he finished saying those words, they heard the master of ceremonies welcome everyone to Memorial Coliseum and announce the names of the teams playing that night—Covington Holmes and Cuba. Amid loud applause, cheerleaders ran out first; then the coaches and their teams walked out and took their places on the benches, all facing the same direction and looking out at the court and the crowd. When the organist began playing "My Old Kentucky Home," everyone stood up, hand over heart, and sang. Then they blew whistles and horns, gave a huge cheer, and sat down to wait for the warm-up to begin. The anticipation of the excited crowd was palpable. All were well aware of Covington Holmes' strength, but only a few knew about Cuba's. This warm-up would give them some idea of the smaller team's ball-handling ability.

If the crowd was curious, the Cubs were jittery. They had never seen so many people, never played in such a huge place. Feeling mounting pressure and excitement, they sat silently, glancing around at the crowd.

Suddenly, the organist began pumping out the jazzy strains of "Sweet Georgia Brown," the Harlem Globetrotters' theme song and, by adoption, the Cuba Cubs.' Jimmy Jones, the team captain, said, "Okay, this is it! Let's run." The crowd laughed as ten Cubs ran onto the court bouncing basketballs painted white, green, and gold to match their satiny new uniforms. It was showtime!

Within moments of the Cubs starting their warm-up by shooting layups, a careless mishap put the game in jeopardy for the team. Taking a routine pass from Joe Buddy, Howie let the ball slip through his hands and hit him squarely in the face. His nose started to bleed profusely. This was the first time ever that Howie had let a ball slip from his hands, and he fought back tears, thinking, Why here? Why now, God?

Fortunately, he got back into action quickly as his team-mates were starting their shooting practice—dribbling, driving, and repeatedly making moves and shots that they would use in the game. Using skills they had learned earlier studying the Globetrotters film and had perfected by hours and hours of practice for three years, they astonished the crowd. Everyone's eyes were riveted on the Cubs as soon as Doodle began to pattern himself after Goose Tatum; Howie, Marques Haynes; Jimmie Webb, Ermar Robertson; and Raymon, Billy Brown. Jimmy Jones, the only senior on the team, had never been shown the Globetrotters film or encouraged to learn any of their techniques, so he played straight-man basketball.

Pandemonium broke out during the shooting drill when Howie erupted into an exhibition of ball handling. He darted around the court like a wizard, dribbling behind his back and between his legs while running full speed. The crowd loved his act and roared with laughter when he paused to dribble the ball with his back end. He moved like a dervish, racing by Doodle, dribbling the ball between Doodle's legs. The basketball stuck with Howie as if it were attached to his hand by an invisible elastic band.

In another phase of the warm-up, the Cubs went into what they called splitting the post. Doodle stationed himself at the free-throw line while the other players, facing him, formed two vertical lines beyond the free-throw circle. Joe Buddy and Howie, the first two players in front of the line, would pass a ball to Doodle as they cut by him quickly. Doodle would roll the ball down one arm, then across his shoulders and down his other arm to make a pass behind his back. Doodle kept feeding the ball in this manner to his team-mates as they ran by him. The crowd squealed with delight watching him fake a pass to one of the Cubs cutting by him and then shoot his windmill hook shot. Passes from Joe Buddy, Howie, and Jim-mie Webb to Doodle were all made the Globetrotters' way—behind their backs and between their legs. During this time they were mov-ing fast. The crowd had never seen a warm-up like this one and showed its appreciation with thunderous applause.

Sometimes Doodle would drop-kick the basketball to one of the two players cutting by him. Other times he would fake to both of them and shoot a hook shot. Occasionally, when Jimmy Jones or Jimmie Webb cut by him, he would put the ball up his jersey and fake a handoff to one of them as they ran by. Then he would remove the ball and uncork his windmill shot, a high looping hook shot that he could sink from twenty or more feet. Fans again roared with delight and chanted with the Cuba cheerleaders: *Hip, hip, hurray! Hip, hip, hurray! Cuba, Cuba, all the way! When you're up, you're up. When you're down, you're down. When you're up against Cuba, you're upside down!*

During the last few minutes of the warm-up, the Cubs went into the five-man weave, demonstrating more complex ball-handling skills while increasing their speed as they weaved about the floor. It was a sight to behold!

For the most part, the Coliseum crowd had never seen high school basketball players handle the ball the way these boys did. With the exception of the invitational tournaments, all of the Cubs' other games in 1950–1951 were played against teams in western Kentucky. Even though they came to the tournament with the best record—winning thirty-three games, losing two, and picked

Cuba cheerleaders: left to right, Barbara Harper, Helen Crittenden, Shirley Wiggins, Julia Harris, and Jackie Edwards. (Cuba School yearbook photo.)

by the *Courier-Journal* to go as far as the semifinals—most basketball fans were not sure they could find Cuba, the place, on a map, or even if they cared to look. However, by the end of the warm-up that night, the curiosity of every person in Memorial Coliseum was engaged. Expecting to see an exciting game, the crowd stood up and applauded Cuba.

The winners of the Ninth Region Tournament, tough mentally and physically, Covington Holmes players had great faith in their own abilities and sneered at Cuba's performance during the warm-up. When the game started, Holmes immediately took charge, making a statement on the lighted scoreboard. The Cubs were nervous and intimidated. They were having difficulty passing and shooting. Hearing the crowd loudly expressing its disappointment with them, they grew even more nervous. They did not even resemble the team that had won the tournament in the First Region. At halftime they seemed hopelessly behind at 21-15.

After the fourth quarter started, the Cubs suddenly sprang into action using an all-court press. They cut into Holmes' lead; the score stood at 34-32. Then Joe Buddy scored on a fast break, his second basket of the game, to tie the score, 34-34, with six minutes left. Next Raymon made his only basket, putting the Cubs ahead, 36-34. Holmes' Al Doherty followed by sinking a free throw, shaving Cuba's lead down to 1 point. The teams exchanged baskets. Holmes made the score 37-36, but then Doodle scored his only basket in the game, which proved to be the winning margin. In the last few minutes, Holmes got the ball twice but failed to score both times. Satisfied with their 1-point lead, the Cubs chose to maintain control of the ball by letting Howie have it. Holmes fouled repeatedly in a desperate attempt to get the ball back, but the Cubs used the available option of taking the ball out of bounds on a foul instead of shooting the free throw. While Howie dribbled until the clock ran out, nearly all of the Coliseum cheered with approval. Cuba beat Holmes 38-37!

Except for the one section filled with Holmes' supporters, the rest of the stadium went wild, standing and cheering with the Cuba cheerleaders, *Two bits! Four bits! Six bits a dollar! All for Cuba, stand up and holler!* Hundreds of large white, gold, and green balloons were set afloat as the organist played "Sweet Georgia Brown." The stadium was on its collective feet, clapping and chanting, "Cuba! Cuba! Cuba!"

That opening-round victory advanced the Cubs to the state quarter finals. The next night, Friday, at 9:15, they faced the huge, highly regarded hometown team Lexington University High. This team had already knocked off Lexington Henry Clay, Lexington Lafayette, and Hughes Kirkpatrick—tough teams to beat—on its path to the state tournament and was not about to slow down now. In addition to being at home, surrounded by friendly fans, University High players were rested, having had the advantages of sleeping in their own beds the night before, eating home-cooked meals, and having no fatigue or other problems that travel often causes. University High had plenty of supporters but—to its dismay—nothing compared to what Cuba had, for by now many of the Bluegrass locals were rooting for the little Jackson Purchase team.

Cuba took the opening tip. Now clearly a favorite with the visiting crowd, Doodle worked in for a hook shot but missed. University High Purples' great rebounding trio of Jimmy Flynn, Aley Harper, and Frank Tilton were living up to their reputations. Flynn connected on a long set shot for the first points in the game. Forward Aley Harper followed with a one-hander before Doodle hooked in a shot, making it 4-2. Doodle later made a free throw, cutting University's lead to 4-3. When Flynn scored on a rebound, he was fouled by Raymon. Joe Buddy went in to replace Raymon before Flynn made his free throw count, putting the Purples ahead at 7-3. The Lexington club seemed to be on its way to victory after Keith Moore banked in a long shot, giving University High a confident lead of 10-3 before Cuba called time-out. University High led by 19-9 after the first quarter. Again, Cuba looked hopelessly behind.

Appearing to be overwhelmed, the Cubs missed most of their shots from the floor. Doodle, who had not played well in the first game, finally pulled himself together and hit three straight Goose Tatum hook shots. Now the score was 23-18. Whenever Doodle made a hook shot, the crowd roared its approval. But the alert Purples were not about to let Cuba get ahead and quickly moved back into a 10-point lead, 31-21. With three minutes left in the first half, Howie scored on a jump shot. Then Joe Buddy cashed in on a rebound just as the half ended, trimming the margin to 31-25.

In the second half, Cuba came back stronger than it had been at any time thus far in the tournament. Howie made two shots; Raymon followed with another; and then Doodle powered in his jump shot, tying the score at 35-35. Once more University High pulled out in front, 39-36, before Doodle evened the score again with only a minute and forty-five seconds to play in the quarter. Purples forward Harper fouled out, but two quick baskets kept University High ahead. Although Howie and Jimmy Jones scored, the third quarter ended with University High leading 45-43. The excited fans clamored for the little "comeback team" Cuba to come on back. They screamed, "Score! Cuba! Score, Cuba! Score!" Unable to sit still, the crowd jumped up and down when Raymon scored off a rebound, driving the Cubs to a 2-point lead. In rapid-fire succession, Howie, Raymon, Jimmy Jones, and Doodle each made baskets, giving Cuba a 10-point lead with three and a half minutes to go.

In those waning moments, University High started fouling in its attempt to get the ball. The Cubs figured they had better lock their lead and gave Howie the ball. As he began killing the clock with a dribbling exhibition, University High scrambled after the ball with increasing desperation. When the game ended, Cuba had won 57-50. Doodle took scoring honors with 23 points, followed by Raymon with 13 and Howie with 11. What a victory it was.

As the players were leaving the building that night, a small boy ran up to Doodle and handed him a program, saying, "Autograph, please." Not understanding what the word *autograph* meant, Doodle looked questioningly at Coach Story who said, "He wants you to sign your name."

The next day, Edd Kellow, sportswriter for the *Paducah Sun-Democrat,* gave a firsthand description of those final minutes: "Then the roof of the entire Coliseum crumbled down on the local lads. For a west Kentucky storm, pent with the fury of a group of kids who had been soundly criticized for being 'overrated,' burst the ball game wide open."

4

The Coliseum Darlings

She [the world] was meant to be wooed and won by youth.
—Sir Winston Churchill

Just hours before the final tournament game was to begin, the governor of Kentucky spoke at a Lexington Chamber of Commerce buffet party held for all the coaches, the board of control, and others involved with the tournament. In a startling announcement, Governor Lawrence Wetherby emphatically but undiplomatically stated, "I'm for Cuba—all the way! The way those kids fight, and just don't want to lose, make sports great. So you take Manual, Clark County, and the rest. I'll just be for those kids from Cuba."

The governor and many others recognized that the difference between the Cubs and their more cosmopolitan contemporaries was not just in their manners, dress, and speech, but in a much deeper sense. The Cubs had a kind of Old World, frontier-spirit ruggedness about them that was distinctive and admirable. The way they persisted, and the way they played and worked together as a team, reflected their pioneer background. Cuba was not a deep team and could not substitute as efficiently as the other teams could. Despite their injuries and illnesses, Cuba's starters played nearly every minute of their games unless, of course, they fouled out—but they knew better than to do that.

More thrilling perhaps than anything else was the way the Cubs' wins came in games where they had to come from behind. Many times when playing a team that was hailed as invincible, the Cubs would trail until the fourth quarter. Then they would burst forth, tie the score, push harder and harder, and get ahead, winning the game just before the final horn was sounded. The Cubs were always determined to win and many times their sheer willpower pulled them through to victory.

Coach Story was a great defensive coach, teaching his team a pressing defense. He developed and nurtured a trust in them that they could go on to win no matter how far behind they were. He had them believing that they would always find a way to get ahead. They won many close ball games with that philosophy; in fact, it became part of their history.

Compelling but nerve-racking to watch was Cuba's apparent style—spot the opponent a lead, wear him down, pull out ahead when he faltered, and then make him play catch-up. Whenever the Cubs were trailing, the suspense in the stadium could be felt as the crowd anxiously watched and waited for the Cubs to spring ahead in the fourth quarter.

Whenever the Cubs got a lead in a close ball game, Coach Story would have them freeze the ball—not shoot, but just keep possession of the ball. This strategy enabled Cuba to win many tough games. In 1951, shot-clock rules did not exist. If a player was an excellent ball handler and had teammates who worked well with him, he could take possession of the ball when his team was ahead and kill the clock, that is, hold the lead until the clock ran out. The Cubs had this technique down perfectly. The reason they were able to perfect it was plain to see.

Although every player on the Cuba team was talented, one of them had a special ability to dribble and handle the ball. With the help of his skillful, unselfish teammates, he could keep the ball away from the other team for long periods. That boy was Howie Crittenden, and it is safe to say that he was the best dribbler and ball handler ever seen in the history of Kentucky high school basketball at that time.

Howie amazed everyone who saw him play. He could handle the ball equally well with either hand while changing speed and direction. He could drive dribbling almost as fast as he could run. He could dribble behind his back and between his legs. He could dribble between his befuddled guard's legs and slip through for an easy basket. This lightning-fast ability gave him many advantages in creating scoring opportunities, in contributing to offensive plays, and in preventing turnovers. The crowd loved to watch Howie get around the defense, break himself loose for quick one-handed shots from the outside, or drive at full speed to the basket for layups.

No one player on any of the other tournament teams captured the crowd's fancy and amused fans the way Doodle did. Doodle's comic exuberance was infectious and his hook shot was astonishing. Irrepressible and irresistible, Doodle loved to make people laugh. And laugh they did—at his behavior, his talk, and his appearance. Although he had a hearty appetite, he was thin and limber as a reed, but muscular. His spiky dark brown crew cut drew attention to his large ears, which fanned out from the sides of his head. He had a little cleft in his chin, and a wide, crooked smile that evoked a smile in return. His brown eyes shone with mischief. When he walked, his long arms and large hands seem to dangle, but on the hardwood, he was a well-coordinated runner. Unlike the others, Doodle never appeared tense or nervous.

His comic manner and constant chatter often threw his opponents off balance. Many times during a game, even an opposing

Charles "Doodle" Floyd. By the time he was a sophomore, Doodle was already able to palm a basketball. (Photo courtesy of Charles Floyd.)

player could not keep from laughing at Doodle's remarks or antics. Like Goose Tatum, he would make a hook shot motion with an empty hand, fooling his opponent and sometimes the crowd too. He would call out to his opponents, telling them what he was going to do. Then he would do it. He pointed out the place on the floor from where he would score and then proceeded to score. No other high school player behaved the way Doodle did. Soon after his first appearance in the Coliseum, he became known as a loveable clown.

Despite his foolishness, Doodle was deadly serious about basketball and hell-bent on winning. His phenomenal hook shot, which made him the top scorer of many games, was compared to that of Cliff Hagan, then playing for the University of Kentucky. Two years older than Doodle, Cliff Hagan had a stunning hook shot that Adolph Rupp said was one of the best he had ever seen. While in high school, Hagan had watched Bob Lavoy, who played for Coach Ed Diddle, shoot a hook shot in a game in Bowling Green at Western Kentucky University. Hagan went home and practiced the shot in his backyard until he had perfected it. People who knew him as a child said that even as a youngster, Cliff played basketball with an unusual grace and precision. From Owensboro Senior High, he went on to play center for the University of Kentucky, where he paired perfectly with Frank Ramsey, a great rebounder, who loved to intercept passes and run the length of the floor.

Doodle was not trying to imitate Hagan. In fact he had never even seen him play. Doodle was just shooting in a way that came naturally to him, and his technique was different from Hagan's. Hagan would position himself on the court, extend his arm way out horizontally from his shoulder, and then toss the ball over his head into the basket. Bewildered defenders took to shaking their hands furiously in his face to prevent him from looking at the goal to shoot. But Hagan was so extraordinarily good at scoring with this shot that he did not have to look at the goal to send the ball down through the net. From his position on the court, he knew exactly where and how to pitch the ball to score. He had perfected his technique to the point that he could make the shot blindfolded.

Doodle's shot was different, yet just as remarkable. Doodle would lean far to his right, stretch his arm straight out, back, and down, using his body to guard the ball. Then he would bring his arm up in a wide sweeping movement and with his arm extended straight over his head so that nobody could get the ball, he would shoot a perfect basket. He could make this shot from a great distance with amazing accuracy. Until they watched Doodle perform this feat, cage fans had never seen any other player shoot in that winding fashion. His shot became known as the Doodle windmill.

Although Doodle and Howie got the lion's share of attention, what made the Cuba Cubs great was the team itself. In no other sport is the blending of talents more important than in basketball. Each of the Cubs was gifted in his own way, and the combination of their talents made them successful. Once Howie got the ball, it was difficult for any opponent to take it from him, but he needed the cooperation of his teammates to work the ball the way he did. Doodle was a great shooter, but without the help of the others, he would not have been able to get his shots. It took the entire team to play and win as they did.

The floor general, Jimmy Jones was a scrappy five-foot-eight guard who had a never-say-die attitude. He helped make the team believe that it could come back no matter what. A good rebounder, he was a key player in the Cubs' comeback wins, stealing the ball from the opposition many times. He also played great defense.

Raymon McClure, the largest boy on the team, weighed about 220 or 230 pounds and was six feet one. Strong and tough, he had a big build for a high school player. His greatest contribution to the team was his rebounding ability. Raymon could block off and

Jimmie Webb could score a lot of points on the basketball court, although there were times he would be so distracted looking around for Martha during practices or time-outs that he missed some of the coach's instructions. (Photo courtesy of Donald Poyner.)

rebound and control one side of the board on defense. He could also pull down key offensive rebounds.

Jimmie Webb, six feet two, was a great outside shooter. He could shoot from thirty-five feet or more. He had a two-handed set shot with a very quick release. It was not unusual for him to hit three or four shots in a row. Jimmie could always score in a clutch and was often the team's next best scorer after Doodle.

Joe Buddy Warren, five feet eleven, was a guard with good ball-handling and defensive abilities. He had a great one-handed set shot. A high jumper, fast and agile, he often performed his assignment of guarding the other team's high-scorer successfully.

Proud of his boys, Coach Story said after they beat University High, "I've really got a first six instead of a first five."

Cuba was not the only little place that had ever captured the attention of state tournament fans, but it was never merely a sentimental favorite, as other small rural teams often were. The Cubs were a favorite in the strictest sense of the word. They differed from other teams in four major ways. First, they played a much showier, more spectacular game than any other team by patterning themselves after the Harlem Globetrotters. Second, they introduced a new style of high school boys' basketball: a much faster manner of playing the game. Although Kentucky high school basketball teams coming out of the 1940s into the 1950s started using the fast break, which made for a more exciting brand of basketball, other high school teams did not handle the ball the way Cuba handled it. Third, Cuba had so many come-from-behind wins that were nerve-racking, gut-wrenching to watch but oh, so thrilling. And, fourth, although the Cubs were showmen, they were, as their opponents discovered, well grounded in the fundamentals. Opponents and fans never knew what to expect from them.

Present in the audience the night Cuba won its second round in the state tournament games was Ed Diddle, coach of the Hill-

Joe Buddy Warren was a key supporting player for the Cubs, although he was not exempt from Coach Story's discipline when word got back to the coach that Joe Buddy had been seen smoking a cigarette. (Photo courtesy of Jimmie Webb.)

toppers men's basketball team at Western Kentucky University in Bowling Green. One of the most successful coaches in the country, Diddle was also one of the best loved and the most colorful. He was noted not only for waving a red towel during every one of his games, but also for his quirky manner of speech. Much to the amusement of his fans, he frequently used what appeared to be unintentional malapropisms. He would tell his players such things as "Line up right here in a circle."

Immediately after Cuba beat University High, Diddle sought out Jack Story. Getting very close to Story and pulling on his coat collar with both hands, Diddle asked him in that manner of speech he was famous for using: "That Crit-ten-ten boy—he dribble that ball like that all the time? And Doodle, he throws that ball like that all that time?" Coach Story laughed, "Yes sir, they sure do!"

The next day, Saturday, at 3:00 p.m., the Cubs played Whitesburg, which had eliminated Danville, 71-44, the day before. Whitesburg's star was Jimmie Bert Toliver, a sharp shooter, who had made thirteen field goals and three free throws—29 points in that game. Somewhat underrated upon entering the tournament, Whitesburg soon proved itself a force to be reckoned with. It had a strong defense that kept Danville's Admirals, a good team, from scoring.

During the opening half, the Cubs were true to form. They fell behind in the first period, then ate away at Whitesburg's lead but trailed 32-29 at halftime. In the second half, Cuba would presumably grind Whitesburg down. But Whitesburg refused to follow the script and instead ran out to a 10-point lead.

Cuba had to fight hard throughout the second half. With one minute left, the Cubs held a 1-point lead. Finally, Jimmie Webb intercepted a Whitesburg pass and threw the ball to Doodle. As he was going in for a layup, Doodle was fouled. He made his first foul shot and then took the ball out of bounds. The Cubs stalled the last few seconds and won 65-62. The fans rose to their feet, blowing horns, throwing confetti, and chanting, *"Cu-ba! Cu-ba! All the way!"*

Despite the afterglow of that game, the Cubs felt a lingering weariness. It had been a draining contest, and they were not a deep team. Howie and Doodle got no rest during games, and the other starters got very little. Playing three tournament games in three days was grueling work. At these tournament games, the opposing teams had substitutes who were nearly as good as the starters. These substitutes were not like the ones the Cubs played in county games, where the Jimmies (a nickname for those who went in as replacements) were no challenge at all. Here at the Coliseum every player was very good.

Before the final game on Saturday at 9:45 p.m. with Clark County, the Cubs had only four hours of rest—not nearly enough time to restore their strength after just playing that exhausting thriller with Whitesburg that same afternoon. Playing on its home court in Winchester, Clark County, a powerful team, had beaten Cuba earlier that year by 1 point. That night the tired Cubs were not up to facing the Cardinals again.

In this championship game, the Clark County Cardinals took off with ease and rolled up a 16-3 advantage. Cuba had lagged behind that far before and come back to win. Fans anxiously waited for that burst of energy that was so characteristic of Cuba, but it just never came. By the close of the first quarter, Howie and Raymon had carved the margin down to 18-10, but the Cardinals were controlling the boards and getting almost all of the rebounds. Clark County led by as many as 16 points in the second quarter and went to the locker room with a 36-23 halftime lead.

The Cubs were visibly weary in the second half. Clark County's players were all larger and taller than Cuba's, and its three star players—Lewis Snowden, Bobo Pelfrey, and Linville Puckett—had played four state tournament games the year before and had ended up in second place to Lafayette. That valuable tournament experience paid them dividends.

Tired and inexperienced, the Cubs were overwhelmed. The Cardinals kept going full steam ahead in the second half, and it was obvious that the little comeback team was not coming back this time. Final score: Clark County 69, Cuba 44.

5

A Vision and an Oath

First say to yourself what you would be; and then do what
you have to do.
—Epictetus

Lexington, Kentucky—March 1951. It was near midnight when the
bus returned the Cubs and their classmates to the Phoenix Hotel
after the closing ceremony ended the 1951 tournament. A gusty win-
try wind, whipping around the street corner, stung their faces as
they stepped from the bus. "Man, it's cold as a well-digger's tail,"
one of them exclaimed as they rushed into the lobby. Instead of following the others, dispirited Doodle and Howie, with their jacket
collars up around their ears and their hands thrust into their pock-
ets, turned and ambled down to the street corner, then stopped
under a lamppost. As they stood there slightly shivering and pon-
dering what to do next, Doodle pulled a tiny silver basketball from
a pocket in his jeans. It was one he had received at the closing ceremony when each Cub had been given a tiny sterling silver basketball
engraved with "Runners-up 1951." To Doodle, that gift was only a

bitter reminder of the great golden trophy that they had lost. He stared at it for a second as it gleamed in the palm of his hand under the glare of the streetlamp. Then he angrily closed his fist, leaned back, lifted his arm up behind his head, and hurled the tiny ball into the black sky with all his might. As he watched it be swallowed up by the darkness and the whirling snow, he muttered something to himself. Then he turned his head to the side, puckered his lips, and propelled a long, dark-brown ribbon of tobacco juice onto the curb. Looking on with disdain, Howie said that it was time to go back to the hotel.

Even at that late hour, the lobby was noisy and crowded with people. Confetti was stuck to hats and coats; green and gold balloons were floating high above heads. A few people were blowing toy horns, laughing, and talking loudly. Many others were somber, quietly bunched together in serious conversations. Bellhops carrying luggage wove hurriedly through the crowd, stopping now and then to answer questions politely. Two or three dozen small children, wearing jelly-bean-colored school jackets, chased each other about the room, laughing as they played with long ribbons of green and gold crepe paper. Some waved little green triangular pennants stamped with *Cuba Cubs* in gold letters, while others waved little red flags stamped with *Clark County* in white letters.

Howie and Doodle paused in the hotel entrance, grateful that no one noticed them. They were too tired to talk. In three days, they had played nearly every minute of four tense tournament basketball games, and they were drained emotionally and physically. Nevertheless, to avoid the crowd waiting to board the elevators, they decided to head to the staircase. Walking up flights of stairs to their room would be better than listening to someone say for the umpteenth time how great they had played and what wonderful sportsmanship they had demonstrated. Then there would probably be some wise guy asking them yet again what it was like to live in Cuba, Kentucky. And now this profound sadness after losing what they had expected to win.

They managed to slip past the lobby crowd without being noticed and made their way to the staircase. It was vacant and cold. A hazy streetlamp pouring light in through a narrow window made the marbled walls and granite steps look bluish-gray. Silently and slowly, they began to limp up the stairs. Each boy was weighed down with thoughts of the recent events: the excitement of their all-day journey to Lexington in their coach's car; the marvel of visiting a big city; the Coliseum itself, like nothing they had ever seen; the strangeness of sleeping in hotel rooms and eating unfamiliar foods; the awkwardness of having to talk to people they had never seen before; the embarrassment of having attention called to their western Kentucky accents and the odd name of their home place. On top of all those things was the indescribable thrill of playing in the state tournament—something they had dreamed about doing since they were eighth graders—and the sheer joy of hearing a gymnasium filled with thousands cheering for them.

After climbing three flights of stairs, Howie felt weak-kneed. He propped himself up against the wall and then just slid down onto a step, saying, "Let's rest!" Doodle nodded in agreement and sat down a few steps in front of him. Neither one spoke for several minutes. Then Doodle, hunched forward with his elbows on his knees and his calloused brown hands cupping his face, began to sob: "Damn it! We should not have lost. We should not have lost." Shaking his head as he rubbed the back of his neck with both hands, he cried out again, "They should not have been that much better than us. No way." And he began pummeling the wall with his fist. His eyes were red and wet when he turned and looked up at Howie. But Howie turned away silently. He did not want to talk about what they should have done or what they could have done. It *was* done. No use talking about it now.

Unlike some other basketball players who were content with just playing in the state tournament, they had gone there to win. When fans congratulated them after the game for being the runners-up, Doodle shook his head and protested sadly, "Oh, no! Being runner-up is not good enough. Near misses count only with horseshoes and hand grenades, not basketball."

At the close of the ceremony, Howie and Doodle were chosen to the twelve-member 1951 All-State Tournament Team and Coach Story was named Kentucky Coach of the Year. Despite those honors and the affection poured out to the boys, nothing could ease their deep sense of loss, not even the fact that newspaper sportswriters and radio broadcasters had changed their view of them. Some of those who at the start of the tournament had said that not much could be expected from the little country outfit were now calling Cuba the most popular, the most colorful, and the most courageous team *ever* to play in the tourney.

When Doodle and Howie got to the sixth floor of the hotel, they saw the Cuba cheerleaders standing at the other end of the hall talking quietly. The moment the girls spotted them, they ran to greet them. With tears streaming down her face, Helen, Howie's twin, wrapped her arms around him and placed her head in the crook of his neck. The other girls, trying to be brave and cheerful, asked the boys to go with them to the party that close friends from Cuba had planned earlier in honor of the team. It was to have been their victory party, one that Doodle and Howie had looked forward to attending because some girls they were interested in were going to be there. But now everything was different, and all they wanted to do was sleep.

Back in their room, they were resting on the two single beds when in walked their teammates Jimmie Webb, Jimmy Jones, Joe Buddy Warren, and Raymon McClure. Their glum expressions prompted Doodle to chuckle and note, in his fisherman's jargon,

"Why, you all look like red worms with all the mud slung out of them." Appearing more dejected than the others, Joe Buddy flung his arms out and let them drop alongside his body, saying that he had left his shoes—Chuck Taylor All Stars—in Spivey's locker. During the tournament, the Cubs had used the University of Kentucky basketball team's locker rooms. Joe Buddy had the privilege of using Bill Spivey's locker. A great athlete, Spivey was the first seven-foot center to play for the University of Kentucky.

Raymon, who had been brooding, stopped eating peanuts, brushed the crumbs off his shirt, and reared back in his tilted chair with his thick legs spread apart. With arms folded across his chest, he looked up and made a rude comment about Joe Buddy's forgetfulness. The two of them began swapping some rank insults until Doodle, stretched out on his back in his underwear, with one arm shielding his eyes, told them to shut up, that they sounded like "plucked hens." He rolled over on the bed, swung his long legs over the side, and sat up.

Leaning forward, he rummaged in the back pocket of his trousers, which were lying across a chair, and drew out a slender book of matches, a cloth pouch of Bull Durham tobacco, and a small packet of thin white paper. He carefully tore off a sheet, laid it in the palm of one hand, and gently tapped out a neat little line of tobacco. Ignoring Coach Story's frequent warnings, Doodle often smoked when he was out of the coach's and his parents' sight. He had become expert, too, at rolling cigarettes that looked just like the store-bought ones he could not afford.

As the others watched and waited, he neatly rolled the paper around the tobacco, licked the edge of the paper to seal it and, with a flourish, struck a match on the underside of the end table and lit the cigarette. Only then did he stand up and make his announcement: "The best thing for us to do now is to quit crying about losing and plan on coming back next year and winning."

Their mood brightened and as they were talking, in walked others involved with the team—Ted Bradley, Charles Wheeler, Jimmy Lowery, Harold Roberts, Paul Simpson, and Jimmy Brown, along with the student managers, Bobby McClain, Mason Harris, and Rex Story. Now that they were all together, they began discussing their mistakes and what they could have done differently. The more they talked the more upbeat they became. They replayed every minute of that last game and saw where they had gone wrong. Summing up their situation, Jimmy Jones reminded the others how lucky they were to have another shot at winning next year and how he wished that he were not a graduating senior. He pointed out that really the only reason they could not hit their shots in that final game was that they all were worn out and perhaps, too, they had allowed themselves to be intimidated by Clark County. Now they had a whole year to get stronger, to increase their stamina, and that was all they needed to do to win the tournament.

Grinning widely, Doodle stood, stretched, and scratched his head. He straightened his shoulders so that he towered over the rest of them. Then with his right hand spread wide open, holding an imaginary basketball, he leaned to the side, stretched his long arm close to the floor, paused, and blew out a loud, long whistling sound through his teeth as he flung an imaginary ball, pretending to make his windmill hook shot.

More cautious and less enthusiastic than the others, Howie shook his head no and reminded Doodle that winning the regional again might not be as easy as making that imaginary shot. He said that they might not have to worry about Paducah Tilghman anymore—its best players would graduate that year—but Lone Oak still had Ken Donaldson, a six-foot center and a sharpshooter, and Sonny Hubbs, a tough guard who could cause a lot of trouble when he wanted to. "And then don't forget," he added, "that Fantastic Phil Rollins is still at Wickliffe."

Raymon agreed with Howie and said that even if they did win the regional games, their opponents at the state tournament would be ready for them next year. "This year they didn't know what to expect. Well, they know now. We won't be able to catch them off guard again. Believe me, they will be getting ready to go back just the way we will. I think Howie is right. This is not going to be as easy to do as you think it is, Doodle."

Still, Doodle insisted that all they had to do was stick together and do what they said they were going to do, and everything would be great. He asked Joe Buddy to hand him the Bible that was lying on the table.

As they had done a few times before when they wanted to make a commitment, they formed a circle, put their arms around each other's shoulders, bowed their heads, and repeated an oath that Doodle, holding the Gideon Bible, made up. They swore to do everything they could to be better players and to get stronger physically. They swore that not only were they going to play in the '52 tournament, they were going to win it.

"After all," Doodle concluded, "that's what Coach Story aimed for us to do all along—win in '52." Jimmie Webb smiled and nodded, remembering the afternoon in 1948 when he, daydreaming in study hall, carved on the underside of his desk "Cuba Cubs—State Champions, 1952."

Howie was exhausted. He got into bed, slid under the sheets, and rolled over onto his side. With his back turned to the others, he pulled the covers over his head and mumbled grumpily that he wished they would turn out the lights and leave. As they were about to go, Coach Story popped the door open and said in a voice as dry as a cracker, "Meet me in the front of the hotel at 7:00 a.m. sharp."

In hardly any time after the other boys had left, Howie was snoring, but Doodle was too excited to sleep. As he lay there softly whistling "Sweet Georgia Brown," he imagined how wonderful it would be at the same time next year when the Cubs won the championship. In his mind's eye, he could see himself on the court, scoring one fantastic bucket after another. He could hear the crowd's thunderous applause as he and the others stepped up to receive the magnificent award. He could see the smiling faces of people in Cuba and Pilot Oak and hear them saying how proud they were of the team. He could hear their cheers as he placed the gleaming trophy in the glass case in the hallway at the Cuba School. "Yessiree," he said to himself, "next year, things will be different."

In the darkened room, while Howie slumbered peacefully, Doodle crept out of bed. Whistling softly, he danced a little jig over to the window, where he stood looking out and listening to the sounds of the city. The place where he and Howie lived had no such sounds.

The moon was shining like a new silver dollar and faint stars dotted the Lexington sky. The electric lights—blinking lights, stoplights, streetlights, neon sign lights, office building and department store lights, billboard lights—all fascinated him. Flicking a switch to turn lights on and off in their hotel room was as fascinating to Doodle then as was flushing the indoor toilet. Neither he nor Howie lived in homes that had electricity or plumbing yet.

Where they lived, nights were lit only by moonlight or lanterns and were filled with sounds made only by tree frogs, hounds barking in the distance, and the gentle tinkling of cowbells from the pasture. Whenever there was a full moon, he and Howie would run up and down the country road near their homes. From a distance, their silhouettes, bathed in the silver moonlight, could often be seen passing a basketball back and forth between them.

6

The Homecoming

There are some defeats that are more triumphant than victories.
—Michel de Montaigne

Early the next morning, silence hung heavily in the Kaiser as Coach Story led the motorcade of supporters home. But that silence was broken just outside of Lexington when much to their surprise people were standing along the roadside waving to them. When they got to Horse Cave, where Coach Story had made reservations for lunch, they were even more surprised to see a hundred or more people on either side of the street in front of the café welcoming them on that cold, overcast day. It seems that after Coach Story made the reservation for lunch, the owner of that café—thrilled to have celebrities in his establishment—called friends from all over Edmonson County to come to Horse Cave to meet the Coach of the Year and his Cubs and also to tell them to pass the word on to others farther along the highway. The coach and the boys were so excited by their reception from the unexpected crowd they hardly ate much lunch.

The tournament games had been broadcast over the radio throughout Kentucky, so basketball fans following high school games knew what a hair-raising fight the Cubs had fought and they loved them.

A few miles west of Horse Cave, the motorcade got on Kentucky 80, which would lead them into Mayfield—the Graves County seat—and then home to Cuba. As they approached each town, they were met by a sheriff or a constable who would lead them through the town. Onlookers parked on either side of the narrow main streets started blowing their horns once they spotted the sheriff's automobile and the big green and gold Kaiser. Stretched across plain wooden storefronts were wide paper banners: "Welcome, Cuba Cubs!" Adults and children stood on the sidewalks, alongside roads, and in front of houses, offices, hardware stores, and other businesses, waving pennants and flags and yelling, "Yea! Cuba!" Dogs ran barking alongside the Kaiser as the Cubs' long outstretched arms waved from the car windows. In some town squares, little high school bands played "Sweet Georgia Brown."

This seemingly endless chain of enthusiastic well-wishers was the result of the efforts of a small group of people in Horse Cave who had initiated a network of telephone calls. The network stretched 140 miles from Horse Cave to Eggner's Ferry Bridge in Aurora, which is in the far western end of the state. No one seemed to mind that the Cubs were runners-up, not winners; they thought of the Cubs as successful. The little team symbolized the hopes and dreams of hard-working, poor people in tiny forgotten communities everywhere.

When they reached Pete Light Springs, east of Kentucky Lake, Coach Story and the boys stared in disbelief at the several hundred cars filled with people waiting for them. Parked along the highway were ten bright, new, different-colored Cadillac convertibles. Automobile dealers from as far away as Nashville, Tennessee, had

A partial view of the crowd that gathered at Eggner's Ferry Bridge to welcome the Cuba Cubs back from their championship win in Lexington. The motorcade that followed the Cubs to Mayfield for a celebration stretched for miles. (Photo courtesy of the *Paducah Sun-Democrat*.)

provided these cars for the players, the coach and his family, the cheerleaders, and the team managers to ride home in.

Carrying the handsome runners-up trophy, Coach Story, Howie, Joe Buddy, and Ted climbed into the first Cadillac. The others got into the following convertibles. With a state patrol car leading the way, the motorcade traveled homeward to Graves County. When they reached Eggner's Ferry Bridge on the Marshall County border about 4:15 on that cold, cloudy afternoon, they saw hundreds more parked cars and a crowd estimated at a thousand cheering and honking horns for them.

Those who did not get to go to the tournament, along with those who did go but returned before the Cubs did, came to Eggner's Ferry Bridge to welcome the team that day. After the crowd greeted the coach and the boys with hugs and kisses, two state troopers led the five-hundred-car motorcade across Marshall County and into

Graves County to Mayfield. By the time the lead automobile got to Hardin, the last car was just leaving the bridge. The motorcade was eight miles long.

None of the Cubs or Jack Story could sit still or face forward in the convertibles. They all kept craning their necks to look back at the train of cars snaking behind them for as far as they could see. Twilight had fallen by the time they crossed the Graves County line. When they arrived at the courthouse square in Mayfield, they were stunned to find a huge crowd (newspapers the next day estimated it at eight thousand). People had come from all over the Jackson Purchase, and they cheered as Coach Story and the Cubs got out of the convertibles. Shaking as many of the outstretched hands as they could reach, Coach Story and the Cubs slowly made their way toward the platform, where a public-address system had been set up and city and county officials and western Kentucky politicians had gathered.

A gentle but cold wind stirred the green and gold crepe paper ribbons and banners decorating the platform. A large United States flag and an equally large Cuba School flag, prominently displayed near the podium, waved softly. The Mayfield High School band, out-fitted in fire engine red uniforms, snappily paraded up to the plat-form, where they played "The Star-Spangled Banner" and "America the Beautiful" as the crowd sang. Many in that crowd that night cried tears of joy and pride.

When Coach Story and the Cubs filed onto the platform, the band burst into "Sweet Georgia Brown," and everyone went wild. The master of ceremonies had a hard time getting his audience to settle down so that he could begin the program. After the superin-tendent of Graves County schools led the Pledge of Allegiance and offered his welcome and congratulations, each of the local digni-taries, the state representative, and the state senator spoke. No one afterward remembered a word of any of the speeches.

When finally Coach Story was handed the microphone, he was so choked up with emotion that he was unable to talk or even to look at the audience. After an embarrassingly long silence, he looked up and around at the crowd and said simply, "Thank you. Thank you. You're the grandest people in the world."

Trying to break the tension, the master of ceremonies introduced each of the Cubs. The boys rose nervously, scraping their chairs back. They looked handsome, dressed in their dark topcoats, suits, white shirts and ties, and real leather dress shoes. Unable to sit still, Doodle leaned closer to Howie and whispered hoarsely, "I feel like I've got a lump in my throat big enough to choke a cow." He no more than got those words out when he was handed a microphone and asked to say a few words. He nervously stammered, "Well, sir, all I got to say is I was scared then and I am scared now. I'm sorry, real sorry, we lost. But I promise we won't lose next year. We won't let you down next year." Then, looking directly at Coach Story, Doodle said to him, "We're going back next year, Coach. Yes, sir, we are going back, and we're going to win that trophy."

Unexpectedly, Joe Buddy jumped up, grabbed the microphone, and shouted, "Yes, sir, we're going back! I left my new Chuck Taylors in Bill Spivey's locker, and I aim to get them back." Laughing, the crowd broke out in thunderous applause.

When the band started playing "Sweet Georgia Brown" again, the cheerleaders hopped up onto the platform, clapping and dancing to the music, shouting, *Cu-ba! Cu-ba! Yes, it's true—State champion in '52!* The crowd picked up the chant and would not stop. The master of ceremonies tried his best to continue the program, but the chanting went on and on. His audience was hearing what it wanted to hear.

7

The Land between Rivers

Men's customs differ; different people honor different practices;
but all honor the maintenance of their own peculiar ways.
—Plutarch

The phenomenal support that Cuba, the Jackson Purchase, and all the rest of western Kentucky gave to Coach Story and the Cubs did not go unnoticed elsewhere in the state. Across the Commonwealth newspapers featured large photographs and articles about the coach, the team, and their incredible reception. Newspapers carried aerial photographs of the automobiles parked near Eggner's Ferry Bridge, of the eight-mile-long motorcade to Mayfield, and of the celebration at the county courthouse square.

A year later, in one of his Sunday morning columns in the *Lexington Herald-Leader*, veteran sportswriter Bob Adair wrote that in the thirty-five-year history of the state tournaments, no team had ever scored a more popular victory than that of "the clowning little Graves County quintet." Musing about the differences between the little team and the local teams, he focused on the remarkable support the Graves County team received, contrasting this with the lack of support the central Kentucky lads got. Compared to the western Kentucky spirit, the local spirit, he said, was deficient. He wanted to know why people in central Kentucky tended to stay at home or to find other ways to entertain themselves rather than attend district and regional tournaments—then, when it came time for the state tournament, they were annoyed to discover the tickets had all been sold.

The Cuba fans, he pointed out, attended their team's games from the beginning of the basketball season to the end, packing every gym in which the Cubs played. In the small rural schools, the gyms would be so crowded that the corners of the court would be rounded off. He added that those fans had to travel some three hundred miles to watch their team play in the state tournament, while many local citizens did not even bother to drive across town. And the few who did, he wrote, ended up booing their local school's team and cheering for Cuba instead. Adair complained that the local team had so little backing that it was embarrassing; except for the school's own cheering section, everyone else rooted for Cuba. It was all very hurtful, he stressed, and especially so when some of the local people yelled insults at the local boys and at the officials and cheered for the Cubs. What made the people in western Kentucky different?

While it is true that the Cubs were disliked by some players on other teams in their area who were jealous of their success, it is also true that when the Cubs went to the state tournament, basketball fans and players were united in their support for them. You could go to the bank with your money on a bet that no basketball fans in western Kentucky would ever root for any team at the tournament other than their own—under any circumstances. "Western Kentuckians," Adair concluded, "are uniquely unified in their commitment to their teams."

Like many others in central Kentucky in 1951 who knew

nothing about the region named the Jackson Purchase, Adair was unaware that it was the residents' geographical location that made them different or, as he said, "uniquely unified."

The Jackson Purchase is a peninsular-looking piece of land jutting out of West Tennessee into the far western tip of Kentucky. Like giant arms, three forbidding rivers wrap around it: the Ohio River to the north, the Mississippi to the west, and the Tennessee to the east. For a hundred years, these rivers cut the region off entirely from the mainstream political and social centers of the state of Kentucky, to which it had been added in 1818. The only land border the Purchase has is on its south side, where it abuts Tennessee, and residents of the region felt more kin to the people there.

When the Purchase became a part of it, the Commonwealth was already twenty-five years old and it went on about its business as if the Purchase did not exist. Until the late 1930s, the political powers in Frankfort largely ignored the region because finding anything other than a registered Democrat in the Purchase was like finding hair on a frog's head. The Purchase still is a Democratic stronghold, but not to the extent it was in the past. With a few exceptions, the Democrats have always had control of the state government. Whenever they had control or were seeking control, they never bothered wooing the Purchase because they saw no advantage in spending their money in an area that they knew they would carry in any election anyway. On the other hand, the Republicans never sought the Purchase's favor either, figuring they would be wasting their time and money.

Until the late 1930s and early 1940s, state politicians, for the most part, directed no funds toward building roads, bridges, schools, or state office buildings in the Purchase, nor did they set up the multitude of semilocal agencies that are part of a state government. Graves County in the late 1940s was given an agricultural extension agency but no facilities or laboratories. Yet the agency in nearby Hopkins County, which is in western Kentucky but not in the Purchase, had a first-class operation. As is the case today, politicians preferred spending state and federal money in counties that had balanced party systems. Politically speaking, you can say that the Purchase disadvantaged itself by adhering strictly to its Democratic stand. Throughout the rest of the state so little was known about the region that the newspaper articles about the Cubs at the start of the tournament differed from the ones at the end, when the *Louisville Courier-Journal* felt obliged to produce an article about Cuba and the Jackson Purchase.

The word *hillbilly* did not accurately describe the Cubs, though they were called that upon their arrival in Lexington, nor did it stick to them long once they were seen playing on the hardwood. Among those they won over with their grace and precision was, as has already been said, Kentucky governor Lawrence Wetherby. Yet, to many of the more sophisticated in the Bluegrass, the Cubs did appear somewhat quaint and countrified. Their temperament and style had been shaped by where they lived. Life in the Jackson Purchase in 1951 more closely resembled conditions in the late nineteenth century than the twentieth. Many of the old ways persisted in the Purchase because the three rivers had for so long kept it geographically apart from mainstream political, cultural, and social centers.

In the early years of the Purchase's history, wagon bridges could not be built over any of the rivers because of their width and water-level fluctuations, and so people in the region grew accustomed to staying within their borders. One generation after another placed great value on tradition. They did not see anything wrong or unusual with continuing some practices in pretty much the same style as their ancestors.

From 1818–1905, no bridges of any kind were built over any of the rivers. Then, in 1905, the Illinois Central Railroad Company built a locomotive bridge over the Tennessee River at Gilbertsville so that passengers could ride the train between Louisville and Memphis. But no vehicular bridges were built over any of the rivers for over a hundred years because no state or federal funds for such construction had been allocated. The first vehicular bridge—the Irvin S. Cobb Bridge—was built in 1929. Stretching across the Ohio River, it connected Paducah, the largest city in the Purchase, to Bridgeport, Illinois. Ferries transporting people and freight over the other rivers were inconvenient or too expensive to use often. Just getting to the ferries was difficult enough because many roads were not paved or even graveled until the late 1940s.

For the most part, the Purchase people had no real interest in crossing any of those rivers anyway. Having been ignored for so long by the state's political and social powers, they felt no attachment to Kentucky, even after the state began to show them some attention. Their kinship was closely tied to West Tennessee. Even after the Eggner's Ferry Bridge across the Tennessee River at Aurora was completed in 1933, finally linking the Purchase to the rest of Kentucky, few took advantage of it.

The Jackson Purchase is part of all that land east of the Mississippi River and north of the Mississippi state line that Andrew Jackson and Isaac Shelby, twice governor of Kentucky, purchased in 1818 from the Chickasaw Indian Nation for $300,000. The larger portion, some six thousand square miles, went to Tennessee and is called West Tennessee; the smaller portion, a little over two thousand square miles, went to Kentucky and is named after Andrew Jackson.

Ancestors of Jack Story and the Cubs were among those pioneers who came to the Purchase in the 1830s. These settlers were common people, escaping hard economic times in the Carolinas, Virginia, middle Tennessee, and central Kentucky. Some historians claim that the personality and temperament of Purchase people is just like that of Jackson, who was called Old Hickory because he was tough as hickory wood. Tenacious and self-reliant almost to a fault, Jackson succeeded sometimes on nothing but sheer willpower. Coach Story used him as a model for teaching the Cubs not to give up and not to make too much of their pain—ever. A stoic himself, Story told the boys Jackson was "a real soldier" who once—without any anesthetic—sat in a chair and leaned on his cane while a surgeon carved a bullet out of his shoulder.

Descendants of the southerners who settled the Jackson Purchase maintained the old southern code of honor—which emphasized loyalty to home place and family, not to the Union or to the state. What Lexington sportswriter Bob Adair and others said was a remarkable display of unified support, loyalty, and pride was simply a reflection of regional difference. Purchase people had a deep sense of place and an independent spirit. As historian Lon Carter Barton put it, "Purchase people used to say they were as independent as a hawg on ice."

They were so independent, in fact, that when Kentucky declared its neutrality in 1861, just after the Civil War started, many of them wanted to separate from Kentucky and unite with West Tennessee to form a new Confederate state. Although this proposal was defeated, more than six thousand Purchase men joined the Confederate military, while fewer than six hundred went to the Union forces. The Purchase paid dearly for being such a Confederate stronghold. Before the war it had been a flourishing district of farmers shipping tons of dark-fired tobacco, smoked hams, bacon, lard, cotton, and wheat down the Mississippi River to market in New Orleans. After the war the Purchase was broke.

Its people grew accustomed to hardships and were oftentimes ignorant of the opportunities offered in the outside world. They were attached to their homes and families and to a simple way of life. They brought their children up the same way they had been reared. Their children and many of their children's children lived and died in the communities into which they had been born without ever having moved away.

When the Cubs' parents were young farmers in the 1920s and 1930s, they had a hard time making a living. That was even before the Great Depression hit in 1933—the year the Cubs were born—when farming fell into an even steeper decline. Although the national economy improved in 1935 and 1936, it bottomed out suddenly in the summer of 1937, and the country spiraled downward into a recession. Lacking electric power, rural areas had no industries to provide jobs, and many farmers, like Howie's and Doodle's dads and Coach Story, left the Purchase for a few years to work in northern factories. Michigan, especially, became a mecca for poor people.

After the Tennessee Valley Authority law was passed in 1933, and the great Kentucky dam on the Tennessee River and the huge lake were created, life in the Purchase was stimulated. With the dam providing hydroelectric plants to furnish inexpensive waterpower, industries located in the region, and the Purchase began to grow economically and socially. Gradually more dams, bridges, roads, and the Purchase Parkway and Interstate 24 were built, thoroughly connecting the region with the rest of the world. Even then, as late as 1951, when Jack Story and his Cubs went to Lexington for the state tournament, much of the Purchase was still backward—socially, economically, and technologically.

But it is a big mistake for anyone to think that the region was Dogpatch, populated with benighted hillbillies. The Purchase produced a good share of distinguished professionals in every area of human enterprise. Among some of its prominent citizens are Nathan B. Stubblefield, inventor of the wireless telephone—the forerunner of the radio; Thomas Scopes of the famed Scopes Monkey Trial; Julian Carroll, governor of Kentucky; and Bobbie Ann Mason, a writer from Graves County. The most famous of all, and the greatest inspiration for the Cuba Cubs, was Alben Barkley, the thirty-fifth vice president of the United States. Born in 1877 in Graves County, he was reared in a log cabin near Lowes, only twenty-four miles from Cuba. Like Howie and Doodle, Barkley was the son of a tenant farmer who barely wrung a scant living from the ground raising dark-fired tobacco. Remembering well what his life was like growing up poor, Barkley did much to alleviate poverty when he was in a political position to do so.

8

The Boys from Graves County

We are such stuff as dreams are made on.
—Shakespeare

When they were small children, the Cubs did not all know one another. None of them was born in Cuba, a hamlet with a population of one hundred or so, but all were from similar small communities in southern Graves County. These little farming communities had developed wherever half a dozen or more families settled. One of the families would open a store bearing its name, and the area would sometimes be named after that family.

Doodle and Howie were born in Pilot Oak, about eight miles from Cuba and three miles from the Tennessee state line. They were nine years old when they forged their strong friendship. Although they were kindred spirits, they were an odd match. Small and thin for his age, with butternut dark-gold hair, Howie was a quiet boy, polite and intense. A serious student, he did well in school. Doodle was taller, heavier, big-boned, and physically strong for his age. He was gregarious, friendly, and good natured. Because of his warm

Joe Buddy Warren, age nine, sports his straw hat as he shows off his new bike in front of one of the houses in which he grew up. (Photo courtesy of Joe Buddy Warren.)

spontaneity and sense of fun, everyone who knew Doodle loved him. But unlike Howie, he was not a good student. He did not like to read or to take time to do homework. School, for him, was more like a social center, a place to meet his friends and to play basketball. Beneath these differences, the two boys had a common and abiding love of play and competition. Local residents became accustomed to seeing the two together, engaged in games that became one long, continuous competition, which extended from season to season.

Joe Buddy Warren was born in Lynn Grove where his father, Jess, started out as a sharecropper. When Joe Buddy was around six, Jess bought a house on a sixty-five-acre farm near Cuba. He farmed until World War II started and then went into the service. During that time, Ina, his wife, worked at the new ammunition plant in Viola, outside Mayfield, the county seat and the only real town in Graves County. After the war, Jess took advantage of the GI Bill, a government program that provided a variety of benefits to veteran servicemen so that they could readjust to society more easily. With his GI loan, Jess was able to buy another farm and some equipment. He also worked part-time at the school for Coach Story. Ina worked at the Merit Clothing Company in Mayfield.

They were one of the few families in Cuba that always had a car and usually it would be a fairly new one. As soon as he learned to drive, Joe Buddy was allowed to use the car. He was the only one of the Cubs who could tour around the county in a nice car. Jess was also one of the few farmers who had a tractor, and he often helped others who needed tractor work done. Joe Buddy lived with his parents and sister in a nice house, small, with a white frame, on the main road, about a half mile from the Cuba School. He entered the first grade at the school in Cuba with two or three others who later became part of the Cubs' team.

Joe Buddy's dad was the only father among the Cubs' parents who encouraged his son to play basketball and the only one who attended all the games. He usually managed the box office and was always available to help Coach Story transport the boys to out-of-town games, and to do whatever else needed to be done.

Raymon McClure was always the largest boy in the class. Folks said he was strong as a bull even when he was a young child. He was older than the others and nearly twenty when he graduated. There was never any nonsense about Raymon, and Coach Story really liked that about him. A hard worker, mature for his age, he lived with his parents and worked on their farm near Sedalia. He attended school

Raymon McClure joined Jimmie Webb as a Cubs player who was married during high school at Cuba. (Photo courtesy of Donald Poyner.)

there until he started the seventh grade at the Cuba School. He married before he graduated from high school.

Another of the starters, Jimmie Webb, lived on a farm in a little place called Wray's, named, of course, after the Wray family who owned Wray's General Store. His dad's farm was close to Pilot Oak, about five miles from the Cuba School. An only child, he helped his father on their sixty-acre farm where they raised tobacco and milked ten cows by hand. Like other farmers who had to have a second job, his dad worked the night shift at the Pet Milk company in Mayfield. His mother's first cousins, Carl and Fred Rhodes, owned Rhodes', one of the two general stores in Cuba. Jimmie attended the Pilot Oak School with Howie and Doodle until the sixth grade. His best friends were two boys who lived down the road from him, and neither one of them played basketball. Jimmie was not that close to his teammates socially—only on the basketball court and on the road to games.

Ted Bradley, usually the first off the bench to replace Joe Buddy, moved from Fulton to Cuba when he was in the fourth grade. A small, dark-haired, dark-eyed boy with a twisted grin, he was full of mischief. He had a good sense of humor and found a similar kind of humor in Joe Buddy, so they were friends from the start. They hunted and fished together and, although they loved basketball, they were not as dedicated to practice as Howie and Doodle were. Ted's dad also farmed a little and worked in Mayfield as a sign painter.

The Kentucky State Department of Education and basketball brought these six boys together in late 1946.

Nearly every little community, even though it was not a town, had its own school, named after its location, and it usually housed twelve grades. Any school with twelve grades was called a high school, indicating that a high school diploma could be earned there. If a child of grade school age said he went to Cuba or to Pilot Oak, everyone knew what school he was talking about. There were no separate programs or institutions called kindergarten or preschool, elementary, middle school, or junior high.

A few of the schools were bricked but most were large, wood-framed buildings with a grammar school on the first floor and a high school on the second. In the rural areas of the Jackson Purchase, as well as elsewhere in the nation, some of these buildings had no plumbing or electricity until the 1940s.

By the late 1930s, the economy in the nation had been so bad for so long that many rural Kentuckians moved to the North to find work. Consequently, enrollment in all of the rural schools was low, and attendance varied. The children had chores or farm duties, so their attendance at school depended on the season, crops, and weather. Many youths stopped going to school entirely, thinking they had all the education they needed by the time they had completed the sixth or seventh grade.

By 1946–1947, the state Department of Education began closing the higher grades (from seven or eight through twelve) in places such as Pilot Oak, Lynnville, and Sunnyside, and began busing stu-

The Cuba School contained grades one through twelve, which was common for rural schools in those days. (Photo courtesy of Donald Poyner.)

dents to one central location—Cuba. This change occurred just as the boys who were soon to become the Cuba Cubs were ready to enter the seventh grade, and the ones who were not already attending the Cuba School had to transfer to it. This twist of fate brought all of them together for the first time, and they became friends by playing basketball together—or, at least, their style of basketball. None of them knew the rules of the game. They made up rules as they played.

Life in southern Graves County was lean and hard and isolated. The one cash crop was dark-fired tobacco, so named because it was flue or fire cured, unlike white burley, which was air cured. Graves County was one of the world's largest producers of dark-fired tobacco. There were few trucks or cars and, in most of the outlying areas, homes had no electricity and no plumbing. There were no picture shows, drive-ins, or televisions, and only a few battery-operated, party-line telephones. An occasional radio, also battery operated, picked up static-shredded broadcasts from the outside world of ball games, boxing matches, caterwauling preachers, and country music. Mostly, there was a lot of time and a lot of outdoors.

The daily rhythm of life was the same in each of the Cubs' homes. By 5:00 in the morning, everyone was up and about, including children old enough to work. Before breakfast could be cooked on a wood-burning stove, the hogs and chickens had to be fed, wood chopped for the stove, and the cows milked, often by the light of a lantern. After breakfast, the men vanished into the barns and fields, and the women went about their work—cooking, cleaning, washing, sewing, canning, and gardening. Every family had a large garden for growing vegetables and fruits that had to be dried, stored, and preserved to feed the family all winter. Although women seldom worked in the fields, they worked very hard tending their vegetable gardens. With the help of their younger children, the women gathered wildflowers, herbs, and blackberries, which grew abundantly on either side of the roads and throughout unplowed fields. No insecticides were used to contaminate the taste of fresh fruit. Herbs were gathered for cooking and for medicinal purposes, and berries for desserts, preserves, and jellies.

After they had done their chores and when school was not in session, children were free to roam. They felt at home no matter where they were. "No Trespassing" signs did not exist. They swam and fished in the ponds; picked blackberries, walnuts, and pecans; and hunted raccoons, birds, squirrels, and rabbits wherever they pleased.

A few boys could always be found playing basketball on the dirt half-courts in front of the stores. Each storeowner kept a basketball waiting for them under his counter because a real basketball was not something that every boy owned. But every stable, tobacco barn, milk house, or outbuilding had some kind of basketball goal, usually a makeshift one made from an old barrel rim, bicycle wheel, or peach basket. If the boys did not have a basketball, they made one out of rags, or they used tin cans for balls.

Basketball is known as the poor boy's game because it does not require expensive equipment or even someone to play with. A boy can practice all he wants, whenever he wants, and for as long as he wants, all by himself. Some Pilot Oak residents can still remember how Howie Crittenden practiced dribbling, oftentimes in the near dark, on a blacktop road between Pilot Oak and Water Valley. He would dribble as much as four or five miles in an evening. After he and Doodle Floyd became friends, they often ran the sixteen miles to and from Cuba and Pilot Oak, dribbling and passing the ball between them. It was their version of a Kentucky basketball fast-break marathon.

9

Little Cuba,
Hub of the Universe

These were thy charms—But all these charms are fled,
Sweet smiling village—Thy sports are fled,
And all thy Charms withdrawn. . . .
And rural mirth and manners are no more.
—Oliver Goldsmith

The closing of the Pilot Oak high school not only brought Howie and Doodle together with Jack Story and the other boys, it made the little place with the strange name *Cuba* the hub of their universe. The connection between the Spanish-held Caribbean island Cuba and this small, remote settlement in the Jackson Purchase is rooted in the region's nineteenth-century exportation of tobacco products.

In the mid-1880s, before the tobacco floors and warehouses were established in Mayfield, farmers had to haul their wagonloads of tobacco to the river closest to them. The three mighty rivers surrounding the Purchase on three sides made that fairly easy to do.

In southern Graves County, farmers hauled their wagons to nearby Hickman to load their tobacco onto packet boats to be taken down the Mississippi River to New Orleans, where an agent would sell it for them. Conscious of their isolation, the farmers looked forward to seeing the men who operated the packets, for they brought news from all the great river towns—Memphis, Natchez, Vicksburg, New Orleans—and from as far away as the British Isles and Spanish Cuba.

The farmers of Graves County could not help but be interested in the island, for it had consistently bought their dark-fired tobacco to make its finest cigars, snuff, and chewing products. When the island became the center of a major international controversy, the farmers' interest was intensified. The action started in February 1854 when Spanish authorities in Havana seized the *Black Warrior*, an American merchant steamer on its way from Mobile to New York. They arrested its captain and crew on charges that the captain had not informed Cuban customs officials of the thousand bales of Alabama cotton he had on board. Although the captain explained that he did not think he had to report the cotton because the cotton was not meant for Havana, the Spanish authorities slapped a $6,000 fine on the steamer and held the captain and the crew in detention.

Upon receiving this news, many American politicians, especially the pro-slavery faction, were outraged. A firestorm broke out, with threats of launching war against Spain. Southern planters, who had long wanted to annex Cuba to the United States so they could expand slavery territory, increase their wealth, and add to their representation in Congress, cast their support in favor of violence. Some moderates also supported war with Spain, thinking that it would relieve most of the internal tension between the North and the South and unify the nation by directing its aggression to Spain. Abolitionists and northerners vehemently objected. Thoroughly agitated and insulted, yet not wanting the United States to invade Cuba, Spain released the captain and his crew and withdrew its charge. It not only repaid the $6,000 fine but gave over $50,000 in compensation to the crew.

The fact remained that U.S. expansionists wanted to own the island. President Franklin Pierce asked his secretary of state to organize a committee of three American diplomats, all of whom happened to be pro-slavery Democrats, to figure out a way to obtain Cuba. In October 1854, the committee met in Ostend, a summer resort in Belgium, and quietly produced a letter that came to be known as the Ostend Manifesto of 1854.

In their negotiations with Spain, the diplomats expressed concern about a possible dangerous slave uprising in Cuba, similar to one that had occurred in Haiti. They argued that such a rebellion would create serious problems in the States. Although that reason may indeed have been one of their concerns, their major objective was to expand slavery to the new territory. At the end of their meeting, they submitted their Ostend Manifesto to Spain. This arrogant document proposed to purchase Cuba, informing Spain that if it acted with "stubborn pride and a false sense of honor" in refusing this most generous offer—which the United States was making to help Spain by buying the island—then the United States had, "by every law human and Divine," the right to take the island by force of arms.

The Ostend Manifesto created another huge commotion in the States and in Spain, and it also created fear of aggressive American expansion in other foreign countries. The foolish idea of going to war for Cuba was eventually dropped, of course, but not until after such intent had been thoroughly exploited by the press.

For either political or commercial reasons—or maybe some combination of the two—a group of men in 1854 in southern Graves County named their settlement Cuba.

Kentucky Highway 303 drops straight south from Mayfield like a plumb line. It was a gravel road until 1949, when the state paved it. If you follow it for about ten miles it leads into Cuba, known as Little Cubie in the late nineteenth and early part of the twentieth century. It was never incorporated into a town, so it never had any defined boundaries. The population count varied according to how far in all directions you wanted to count as Cuba. If just the people who lived in close proximity to the two stores, the two churches, and the school were counted, then the population would be very small, maybe fewer than fifty in the early 1900s. While the Cubs were growing up in the 1930s and 1940s, about twenty-eight families lived in small houses in that area. A few other families claiming Cuba as their address lived in more isolated areas, at the ends of dirt roads, and miles apart from each other.

Driving into Little Cubie in those days, you would have a sense of a very pleasant place—one that was steadfast and secure, where life was slow, where nobody ever got into a hurry. Hattie Page Glenn, oldest daughter of the Graves County physician Marion Page, grew up in Cuba during the 1920s and 1930s. She explained, "Nobody had anywhere to go. The people lived simple, self-sufficient lives. They grew what they ate and made what they needed. Their motto was 'Make it do or do without.' The rest of the world could have fallen away, and they would have survived."

Cuba was a closely knit community of the descendants of those who had settled there in the 1850s. Most of the surnames of people who had lived in Cuba in the early period of its history were still represented in the census rolls of the 1940s. That fact made it a cohesive place: in politics (all were Democrats), in economics (nearly all were farmers), and in education—all had attended the Cuba School and all sent their children to that school. The school was the glue that held the community together.

The people knew each other by first names. They looked after each other and each other's children, and they swapped work. In the fall they got together to cut tobacco; in the winter, to kill hogs; in the spring, to plant crops. When it came time to thresh wheat, all the farmers and the one who owned a power-driven thresher would go from farm to farm until all the threshing was done. Whenever a man needed to build a house or a barn, his neighbors helped him. No one paid for labor for those building projects, only for lumber and supplies. The women and children often went along to serve huge meals prepared earlier that morning, turning the end of the workday into a social event.

When the Cubs were growing up, Cuba had one physician—Dr. Marion Page. He served nearly all of southern Graves County. He started out making house calls in his horse-drawn buggy and then in an automobile as soon as he could afford to buy one. Also, Cuba had one blacksmith, two cemeteries, two general stores, two preachers, and two churches—one Baptist, the other Church of Christ. And that was all.

Cuba never had a courthouse, jail, post office, café, bank, funeral home, drive-in theater, sidewalk, streetlight, or even stoplight. It never had a mayor, judge, constable, magistrate, policeman, or sheriff. It did not need any of those officials except on the rarest occasions; then the sheriff from Mayfield came to take care of the problem. It had nary a lawyer, either. A man's handshake sealed a contract. Cuba was mostly peaceful, not like the nearby area around Dukedom, near the Tennessee line, where everything from drunken fistfights to fatal stabbings and shootings went on routinely in the vicinity of a large moonshine whiskey still that operated behind an abandoned building.

Cuba's two general stores were gathering centers, built directly across from each other on its main road—Highway 303. Opened in 1936, Harper's was owned by Jack and Pauline Harper. Their daughter Barbara Ann was in the Cubs' class and was one of the cheerleaders. She and her mother were popular, and so many children and their mothers liked to visit at Harper's.

The other store, Rhodes', dated back to the 1850s and originally stood off the main road. It was a huge, white-framed, two-storied, boxlike building owned by brothers Fred and Carl, who had inherited it from their father. In 1940, Carl and his wife, Opal, constructed a new store right across the road from Harper's and closed the old one. However, no disputes or competition existed between the two storeowners, and though Rhodes' carried more products than Harper's, the village folks traded at both places regularly.

People who lived closest to the main road tended to go to Rhodes' every afternoon after the rural mail carrier had come. Until the mid-1930s, the "post office," built in front of the store, was nothing more than a huge wagon wheel with boxes nailed to it. Each box had the name of its owner painted on it. At the bottom of the wheel were two other boxes. One contained outgoing mail. The other was a large community box that held catalogues, books, newspapers, magazines, and perhaps a few letters to those who seldom received any mail and so had no individual box.

In the early 1940s battery-operated radios lifted the entertainment level in the stores to new heights. Every afternoon children gathered to listen to *The Lone Ranger* and *Jack Armstrong—The All American Boy*. In the evenings, the adults listened to news relayed by Walter Winchell and other such notables. Then they enjoyed listening to such programs as *Amos and Andy, Lum and Abner, Red Skelton, George Burns and Gracie Allen,* and later on *The Bing Crosby Show*. The highlight of the week was Saturday night when the *Grand Ole Opry* would come in over WSM from Nashville.

Until the mid-1930s, out in front of both stores were rails for hitching horses and horse-drawn wagons; two gas pumps were added later. In the yards behind the stores were barns where chickens, hogs, eggs, corn, molasses, fresh vegetables, and anything else that had been brought in and traded for goods were stored. For the most part, farmers traded their fresh produce and dairy products for canned foods and staples, such as flour, cornmeal, sugar, and coffee. Cash came from the city folks from Mayfield, Murray, and Fulton, who shopped in the country stores regularly for fresh eggs and produce.

"Store setters," septuagenarians and octogenarians, moved back and forth between the stores every day, visiting and joking with the customers and teasing the children. In the summer, these old men sat on the store porch, and in the winter inside around a pot-bellied coal stove. All were pipe smokers with teeth worn down from years of clenching pipe stems. They talked, laughed, and played checkers with Coke bottle tops. Howie and Doodle loved to beat them at their own game. Doodle always created some kind of comic hubbub trying to cheat at checkers.

These stores were one-stop shops. They carried everything that anybody needed or wanted. They sold not only food but also clothing, hardware, seeds, farm implements, building materials, saw blades, Octagon soap, bolts of colorful material and sewing notions, and a few patent medicines such as Lydia Pinkham's Vegetable Compound for Female Complaints. Each store had a cold drink box for "pops." Near the cash register, at a child's eye level, was a large glass jar full of candy. Against the walls, sacks of flour and cornmeal were stacked next to wooden barrels of vinegar, sugar, and coal oil. The stores smelled of a mixture of scents, from the brine in the pickle barrel to the licorice and peppermint sticks in the glass jars on the counter.

Huge blocks of ice kept cold the meat counters, filled with fat rolls of bologna, blocks of cheddar cheese, and sometimes freshly caught fish. Thick bologna and cheese sandwiches, popular items, were made to order. Often before games, Doodle and Howie ate such sandwiches for their supper. On top of the meat counter sat three big round glass jars: one filled with crackers, another with pickled eggs, and the other with pickled pigs' feet.

Those families who lived in houses at the end of dirt roads in the woods could not get to the general stores often. For them, Tom Floyd's "rolling store" was a welcome sight. His store was a horse-drawn wagon loaded with many of the items the general stores carried. In addition to dry foods, he had bolts of material, dress patterns, needles, threads, and bobbins for the old treadle sewing machines. In his wagon were shelves separated with compartments jam-packed with different kinds of items that a housewife might need. The top of the wagon held cages filled with clucking chickens and ducks, and also harnesses and farm tools. From the back sides of the wagon dangled galvanized pots and pans. Tom Floyd had a big set of scales, a few spices, and some candy that he gave freely to delight the children.

Tom Floyd was Doodle's great uncle, and Doodle and his sister Lillian loved riding with him to Mayfield to buy stock for the wagon. Then, back at his house, he would let them weigh the flour, sugar, and cornmeal in white paper bags. Doodle did the weighing and Lillian, with her nice penmanship, labeled the sacks. Tom made his living traveling four routes each week around Cuba, Pilot Oak, Lynnville, Dukedom, and Water Valley. His code of ethics prohibited him from ever going closer than one mile to a store. After the Ford Model T truck became available, Tom retired, while other rolling store owners moved their wagons onto the top of the trucks and continued to motor about the countryside peddling their wares.

Depending on the weather, the roads were dusty hard dirt or sloppy mud. Surrounded by large shade trees, some of the houses were built far back on their lots to avoid the dust. Nearly every house had a front porch with a swing. In the evenings folks sat on the porches or strolled to the stores and visited there. Aware of their isolation, they welcomed visitors and ideas from outside the Purchase.

Thomas Floyd and his rolling store traveled throughout the community. This picture was taken after he retired, so there is no merchandise shown on his wagon. (Photo courtesy of Charles Floyd.)

Almost every home had some books, daily newspapers, a Farmers' Almanac, a few magazines and catalogues. Women enjoyed periodicals such as *McCall's* and *Ladies' Home Journal.*

Different levels of the social spectrum existed in Cuba, as they did everywhere else. Some people had a little more money than others, and some had more education, but a person's identity was earned, not inherited. A man was not judged by his ancestry or bank account. He was judged by how hard he worked and managed his business, by how fairly he traded, and by how well he took care of his family and got along with his neighbors. If he could bind a hand of tobacco leaves quickly and neatly, if he could train animals without being cruel to them, if he took pride in his place and kept it nice, if he was good to his family and faithful to his wife, if his children were well-mannered and industrious, if he was honest—paying his debts and keeping his word—a man was respected. His word and his handshake were all that was needed to legalize an agreement. Women were judged by their loyalty to their husbands, families, and God; by their ability to have children and raise them well; by their thriftiness and the quality of their culinary, housekeeping, and sewing skills. These simple values were cherished and instilled in children and passed down from one generation to another. No one in Cuba ever felt a need to lock a door.

10

Doodle Floyd

> A boy's will is the wind's will, and thoughts of youth
> are long, long thoughts.
> —Henry Wadsworth Longfellow

Pilot Oak, Kentucky—1932–1948. From the time he was six until he graduated from high school in Cuba in 1952, Doodle lived with his parents in a three-room unpainted house on a forty-five-acre farm. It was just off the Pilot Oak–Dukedom road, close to the Tennessee state line, three miles from Pilot Oak. His dad paid $800 in cash for the property, using money he had earned as a carpenter-millwright setting machines and turbines in Detroit, where he worked three to four months every winter for years.

Until he bought his own land, Doodle's father worked on the Johnny Morris farm. Mr. Morris provided a small house in the backwoods about a mile out of Pilot Oak for the Floyds and their seven children. Weatherboarded on the outside, it had a tin roof, three rooms, and three windows. Doodle was born in this house on April 23, 1933, the last of the six sons born to Lexie Belle Jackson and

Doodle's mom, Lexie, was a hardworking farmer's wife. (Photo courtesy of Charles Floyd.)

Vodie Carnell Floyd. A year younger than her husband, Lexie was thirty-seven years old when Doodle was born.

Christened Charles Kenneth Floyd, Doodle got his nickname when he was about four and his dad teased him about playing with doodlebugs. Doodle entered this world as a main attraction, weighing nearly fifteen pounds. Neighbors who came to see him the day of his birth said he looked like a three-month-old child. Old Dr. Bard, from Wingo, said Doodle was the biggest baby he had ever *caught* (a term country doctors used for the word *deliver*). All the Floyds were well over six feet tall—big boned, lean, and strong—so Doodle's size was no great surprise.

His five older brothers were William, Herschel, Harold, Hobert, and James, the youngest, three years old when Doodle was born. Harold died of blood poisoning in 1927 at the age of ten. Lillian Beatrice, Doodle's only sister, was thirteen years older than he, and she looked after him and James. She worked hard helping her mother. From the time she was seven until she left home at sixteen, Lillian missed school every Monday to help her mother wash clothes.

Doodle wore clothes and shoes passed down from his brothers until he was a junior in high school. Once a year, everyone in the family got a new pair of shoes to be worn only to school and to church. At all other times, the children wore whatever shoes the older ones had outgrown. Most of the time, the small children went barefoot, unless it was too wet or too cold.

When Doodle was about three, Mr. Morris fired Vodie after an argument about crop division. Morris thought that Vodie had cheated him, even though it was generally known that that was not true. Vodie Floyd was honest and hardworking. The argument was unpleasant and humiliating, but sharecroppers were often the objects of humiliation. With seven children and a wife to feed, Vodie took the first job offered to him and went to work on the old Roland place, near Water Valley, where conditions were better and the house much nicer.

The Floyds lived on the Roland farm until 1939, when they bought their own place: forty-five acres that included a small, dilapidated house, an old tobacco barn, a henhouse, an outhouse, and a smokehouse. Lexie and Vodie slept in the living room, and the older boys shared the two double beds in the other room. While Doodle was still a toddler, Lillian slept on a cot alongside him on the closed-in back porch.

His dad and brothers loved sports and talked about them often, so early on Doodle got the idea of how wonderful it was to excel in sports. He, his dad, and James listened to the boxing matches on the radio. They walked by lantern light to Jess's house, their nearest neighbor two miles away, to listen to special events on his radio. They all especially admired Joe Louis, who dominated the heavyweight division from 1937 to 1949. On their walks to and from Jess's house, Vodie would hold the lantern while James and Doodle danced and pranced like boxers, playfully punching their fists at each other. That night in 1937 when Joe Louis knocked out James Braddock in the eighth round, Vodie decided he had to have a radio of his own. Next day, he ordered a Philco from a *Sears, Roebuck & Co. Catalogue.* Waiting for it to arrive in the mail created much excitement in a family that had so little, for the children had no toys, games, or books other than schoolbooks.

Vodie placed the new radio on the table near his rocking chair and ordered the boys not to touch it. He did not want the battery to run down. Every day as they ate lunch, they listened to the news and then to *Midday Merry-Go-Round,* a country music program featuring such guests as Tennessee Ernie Ford, Roy Acuff, and Minnie Pearl. After lunch, Vodie always rested for a full hour, listening to the music show. He believed in letting the plow mules rest for an hour at midday, too. Then the radio stayed off until he returned for supper and to listen to the news and the commentators—H. V. Kaltenborn, Gabriel Heater, and Lowell Thomas. Sometimes, though, after his father left in the afternoon, Doodle would turn the radio on low and switch the station to some program he wanted to hear. He never quite succeeded in resetting the dial exactly where his dad had left it. His dad always knew that Doodle, not James, had fiddled with it and would bark, "Doodle, keep your hands off this radio!"

Left to right: Hobert Floyd, age fifteen, James Floyd, age twelve, and Doodle, age nine, standing beside the Model A Ford their father, Vodie, had just bought in Detroit. Somebody else drove it back to Kentucky for him because he hadn't yet learned how to drive. (Photo courtesy of Charles Floyd.)

In 1943, with the help of Jess, his neighbor, Vodie finished building a new house for his family, right next to their old house. It took three years to build and it fulfilled, at last, Lexie's longing for a place of her own. This new house had four large rooms and each room had two large windows. Although the house was not insulated, it had double walls so it stayed warm during the winter. Vodie shingled the roof instead of using tin, and he covered the floors with linoleum. To Lexie's further delight, he even made screen doors and hung screens on all the windows. The house had no running water or electricity, but he bought a couple of the newfangled lamps called Aladdins, the next best thing then to electric lights. Unlike the old kerosene lamps that lit up only a small area, the Aladdins, with their net-shaped cones inside the dome, actually spread light out over the entire room.

By the time this house was finished, Bill, the oldest child, had enlisted in the armed service, and Herschel, Hobert, and Lillian, at sixteen, had all married and moved away. Only James and Doodle were still at home. They were inseparable companions and great friends.

The Floyds' place was in the woods, three miles from Pilot Oak. There was no road to it—merely a dirt lane, two and a quarter miles long. No cars, milk trucks, or ice trucks could travel it. Hard rains would wash gullies so deep that the lane was difficult even to walk down, much less to drive a wagon over. Vodie always packed dirt back into these gullies when the earth dried out, so that he could use the wagon. Despite the shape it was in, Doodle and James traveled the lane several times a day, every day, as they went about their chores.

Until Vodie sold the cows, tending the cows was the brothers' biggest responsibility. First thing every morning, the boys would go to the barn, feed the cows, and prepare to do the milking. They had to hold the two-gallon milk buckets between their legs tightly or else the cows would kick the buckets over. Sometimes the boys' legs would get so tired they quivered uncontrollably. As the boys milked the cows, four cats, waiting for their breakfast, sat on the windowsill. Now and then the boys would aim a cow's teat toward a cat and shoot a thin stream of milk to it. The cats caught the milk shot every time.

After the morning milking, the boys would let the cows into the pasture to graze until late afternoon. In the evening, they would herd them back into the barn to feed and milk them again. In the summer, the boys lowered the cans of milk into a large vat they had filled with cool water, hauled from their cistern or from the underground icehouse in their backyard. Without refrigeration, it was very difficult in the summer to keep milk from spoiling.

Before daybreak every morning, the first sound from the main road would be the clattering of the empty galvanized cans on the Pet Milk company truck coming from Mayfield. The truck driver would collect the freshly filled milk cans and leave clean empties for the evening milking. He drove from farm to farm wherever it was possible to drive. Farmers who lived at the end of narrow lanes, as the Floyds did, had to haul their milk cans down to the main road so the truck could pick them up. Every morning, James and Doodle had the difficult job of hauling the heavy full milk cans in a large wheelbarrow with a steel wheel down the lane to the main road. Rolling the empty cans back to the barn was no problem, and they, eager to have their breakfast, ran doing that.

At noon every Monday, Wednesday, and Friday, the ice truck left the Floyds a hundred-pound block of ice on the main road for the boys to take home. Carrying that heavy block of ice was not easy either. James would grab one end of the burlap sack, Doodle the other, and off they would go. They took turns being lead man because he got the back of his legs and his ankles less banged up by the ice. In just doing their chores, Doodle and James walked eight to twelve miles a day every day, except Sunday. This sustained labor amounted to a program of strength and endurance training.

In the afternoons, they were free to do what they chose. James usually stayed home to help his mother, to whom he was devoted. Doodle went to Pilot Oak to find Howie and to see if the older boys would let them play a game of basketball with them. In the early 1940s, Robert Wagoner, four or five years older than Doodle and Howie, had smoothed a dirt half-court across the street in front of his dad's store in Pilot Oak. He had cut down and trimmed a small tree to make a post upon which he nailed a backboard and a real goal. After that he bought a new basketball from the sporting goods store in Fulton. As small boys, Howie and Doodle used to watch Robert and his friends play and eagerly wait for an invitation to join them. Once the older boys realized how good the younger two were, they welcomed them into their games.

Later, when they were playing basketball for Coach Story,

Howie and Doodle would have had a hard time getting to and from the Cuba School for games had it not been for Robert. On many nights, Robert drove them to Cuba and then back home again; otherwise they would have had to walk. Coach Story never came after them, and their parents never drove them to the school. For a long time, the Crittendens did not even own a car.

When Howie and Doodle were not playing ball, they were running. Running was free and easy. They could go as far and as fast and for as long as they wanted. Howie was built for speed. The muscles of his legs were tapered and hard, ideal for a runner. He ran so fast he sometimes looked as if he were airborne. Gangling and awkward-looking, Doodle did not look like a runner, but he was a powerful one. Often in the long, unhurried days of summer, the two boys would race to Cuba and back, a distance of sixteen miles or so. Their ability as runners later gave them an advantage on the hardwood, where they played a fast game, running up and down the court, sometimes keeping the ball from even touching the floor.

Although other children would start out playing tag with them, no matter who was tagged, Doodle would always end up alone chasing Howie, the fastest runner of them all. Many times their race would last all day until dark. With their heads held firm and straight, and their feet rising off the ground as if they were touching hot coals, they would run for miles around Pilot Oak. When they got tired, they would sit under a shade tree and rest— maintaining between them whatever distance Howie had earned over Doodle. If Doodle began to sneak in closer, Howie would take off again.

They were often seen running up and down the main road in Pilot Oak pretending they had a basketball and tossing it between them. They were so in sync with each other that they could make all their fancy moves and work out all their routines with nothing more

Even at fourteen Doodle could be quite a charmer. (Photo courtesy of Charles Floyd.)

than their imagination. No other boys in the area played as earnestly as they did, nor were others ever interested in playing with an imaginary basketball. Old folks enjoyed watching the two boys run, jump, dribble, shoot—all without a ball—but they often wondered aloud "if those two would ever amount to anything!"

11

Howie Crittenden

God tempers the wind to the shorn lamb.
—Henri Estienne

Howie and Helen, his twin sister, were born on March 13, 1933, in Pilot Oak, to Willie and Alta Ruth Crittenden. They were the youngest of ten children. Alta was forty-one years old—far too old, the other women said, to have another baby, much less two at one time. The twins must have been a big surprise for Willie and Alta Ruth, for they came along at a time when she thought her child-bearing days were over. Norman, their youngest, was nine years old when Alta Ruth became pregnant with the twins. Her pregnancy was an uncomfortable one; her belly, some said, got as big as a barrel. An old neighbor woman and Dr. Page delivered the twins in the Crittendens' home. Each baby weighed over eight pounds at birth.

Older than the mothers of the twins' friends, Alta Ruth looked even older than her age. She was tall and gaunt with limp brownish-gray hair and soft brown eyes. Her complexion was dark and leathery from years of working outdoors. She had a way of tucking her head down toward her right shoulder as if she wanted only the left side of her face to show. A wine-red birthmark that began in her hairline and went down one side of her face, covering most of her right eye and her right cheek, made her self-conscious. She tried to conceal it by wearing her long straight hair parted on the left and pulled down slightly over the right side of her face. She plaited her hair into one long braid, tied the end of the braid with a piece of twine, and laid it over her right shoulder. When she was younger, she often placed a wildflower in her braid.

Childhood polio had crippled Willie Crittenden. His legs were twisted, with one three inches shorter than the other. Although a severe limp caused painful back problems, he worked without complaining. Willie Crittenden had no knowledge of or interest in athletics. For as long as everyone in Pilot Oak could remember, Willie complained about his youngest son wanting to play basketball all the time. The boy, he grumbled, never wanted to help him in the tobacco field. It was not until Howie's junior year in high school that Willie went—one time only—to see his son play ball. The only reason he went then was all the talk in Pilot Oak about his son's remarkable athletic ability. He wanted to see it for himself.

Alta Ruth showed no more interest in her son's passion for basketball than Willie did. She never saw Howie play any of his high school games. But by the time he got to be a junior and had made a name for himself as a great athlete, she bought a radio and listened to the Mayfield station broadcasts of the games. Perhaps Howie's parents did not attend games because they rarely had a car and were too proud to ask anyone for a ride. Whatever their reason, it is hard to explain why they never gave their son any praise, any sign of appreciation, or any encouragement to continue in sports.

While his ten children were growing up, Willie farmed, although he was never successful at it. From the time the twins were born until World War II started, he worked as a sharecropper, moving his family several times from farm to farm in and around the Cuba–Pilot Oak area. During the short period they lived in Cuba, he worked as a janitor at the school. But he did not like working inside and returned to farming, raising corn, sweet potatoes, and tobacco. Life was never easy for him or his family.

Alta Ruth worked outside as hard as any man ever did. Every year she planted a large garden and canned many jars of vegetables and fruits, enough to last her family until the next summer. When she was lucky enough to have a cow, she made butter and cheese. She also made most of her family's clothes and all of their quilts by hand from scraps of cloth cut from old clothes.

It is not hard to imagine how sad and helpless Alta Ruth must have felt most of her married life, especially when she and her children had to move into a flimsy three-room dwelling that had holes in the walls and floors. One particularly cold winter when the twins were about three, the Crittendens nearly froze to death. The wind and snow blew in through the cracks, and the holes in the floors invited invasions of rodents. Howie recalled seeing his distraught mother sitting on a stool one morning crying after she had discovered that a rat had bitten the toe of her oldest son, W. A.

Their house was no different from many others that sharecroppers were forced to live in. Sharecroppers had no alternatives—indifferent, out-of-town landowners provided nothing better for them. Even as a small child, Howie believed that life could and should be much better than the one he and his family were living, and he was determined to make a better one for himself. He often thought about what Coach Story had told him and the others about how playing basketball really well would help them earn scholarships to colleges. With a college degree, the coach said, they could get good-paying jobs and have a good life.

When spring finally arrived after that particularly harsh winter, Willie took a job on another farm in a more isolated area where the owner provided a little better house. When the weather permitted, the twins would play in the fields, gullies, and ditches around their house. With no other children to play with, Howie and Helen became inseparable. Their only other playmate was their solid-white dog, a part collie they named "Collie." She ran with them everywhere they went, and she protected them from snakes. They had no toys other than their "Tom Walkers"—stilts that their older brother Norman made for them. When they got tired of these, they would spend hours on summer afternoons making frog houses by covering their feet with mud and then standing perfectly still till the mud dried, then carefully slipping their feet out. Play, for them, required being inventive.

From the time he was small Howie liked to compete, and as a result he got into more accidents than his other siblings. His dad said Howie was "showing off all the time." One such accident occurred soon after W. A. gave the twins a new red tricycle for their fifth birthday. It was the first present they had ever received. They took turns riding it around the yard. Howie loved riding fast down a steep hill where the yard sloped toward the dirt road. Trying to get more speed than Helen had done, he rode that tricycle down that hill without putting his feet to the pedals. Abruptly, he hit a rock, flipped over, and broke his left arm.

When his mother saw his arm, she knew that the break was a bad one—one that only Dr. Page could set. She grabbed a basket of eggs, ran to the barn, and hitched the mule to the wagon. With Howie crying and begging not to go, she and Helen sat silently in the wagon the nine miles to Cuba. Having no cash, she gave Dr. Page the eggs for payment.

There was never any money in the Crittenden household, even for necessities such as medical care. Two of the children died as infants, probably from a lack of medical attention, as was, tragically, common at that time. Alta Ruth used folk remedies to treat her fam-

Howard "Howie" Crittenden, Mr. Cuba High. (Photo courtesy of Howard Crittenden.)

ily. When Howie was six, he cut his foot badly on a dirty piece of glass. This was before tetanus shots and antibiotics were available, so his mother applied the standard remedy of her time and place: she poured coal oil into the wound and wrapped his foot with clean rags until it healed.

It was a common practice in rural areas like Pilot Oak and Cuba for mothers to enroll their five-year-olds in the first grade. In late summer 1938, just before the twins were to enter the first grade, Helen came down with the flu. Howie refused to go to school without her, and Alta Ruth did not make him go. Then when he got the flu, Helen did not want to go without him. Both had missed so many days that they had to repeat the first grade. That put Doodle, Jimmie Webb, and Joe Buddy, who were the same age as the twins, a grade ahead of them, at least for a few years—until those boys each failed a grade.

At school that first year, Howie got his first taste of recognition, and he loved it. When the teacher offered a prize to the student who colored a picture the neatest, Howie took her offer more seriously than the other children and won the contest. The teacher rewarded him with a piece of candy, two toy soldiers, and words of praise.

When the twins were in the second grade at Pilot Oak School, Howie participated in the field-day activities. Later, he said this experience gave him an understanding of what it means to compete. From the day the teacher first explained field-day races, he started training to win. Every afternoon he ran barefoot up and down the gravel road in front of his house, which was across the road from the school. He lost the race that year, but he won every year after that.

It was also in the second grade at the Pilot Oak School that he discovered basketball, for Pilot Oak had an exceptionally good team that year. Twice a week, the first, second, and third graders were permitted to watch the high school team practice in the gym, though they never got to see any games. Howie loved watching the players. When he went home in the afternoons, he would try to imitate what he had seen the older boys do. A previous owner of the Crittendens' house had nailed a large tin molasses can on the side of the smokehouse and had left a rubber ball about the size of a tennis ball in the smokehouse. Howie spent hours tossing that ball through this tin can. Soon he was able to shoot the ball through the can from a little distance. When the ball split from age and use, he filled it with rags and kept playing. He played alone, for by now Helen was more interested in her schoolbooks and in helping her mother. It was not until he met Doodle that Howie found someone who challenged him athletically.

The Crittendens went through many hard times, but the cruelest were from 1937 to 1942. The nation was in the throes of a recession, and the Crittendens were among many who were ill housed, ill fed, and ill clad. By the spring of 1940, all of the Crittenden children except the twins had moved to Detroit and were working in factories. Willie was left with only seven-year-old Howie to help him finish getting his crop in.

To get to his tobacco patch, Willie had to walk nearly a mile through a pasture that had several cows and a Jersey bull. This bull had horns and weighed nearly a thousand pounds. His coat had a beautiful dark sheen, which meant he was at least five years old. The older bulls get, the meaner they are. This bull was devilish and moody, often going ferociously after horses, mules, and men. Then, on occasion, he would act as docile as a rabbit. Howie dreaded going across that field and pleaded with his father, but Willie made him go, saying that old bull was not the worst thing he would ever have to deal with.

Every year Willie planted sweet potatoes, tobacco, corn, and an acre of peanuts. Little did the family realize that it would be the peanuts that would get them through one winter. Hard rains that summer turned the fields into mud. The tobacco and the corn rotted. Only the sweet potatoes and the peanuts survived. Likewise, Alta's garden did poorly. Once the sweet potatoes and all the food that Alta had canned the previous year had been eaten, only the peanuts were left. She roasted, parched, and fried them. The Crittendens ate peanuts every day all that winter long. Their charge account at Wagoner's was already more than they could pay, and they were embarrassed to ask the owner, Fred Wagoner, for more credit. Without cows, corn, or chickens, they had nothing to trade.

Farmers had not shared in the nation's general prosperity during the 1920s. During the Great Depression of the 1930s, many big farms had been subdivided or sold so their owners could pay taxes. Although the economy improved between 1935 and 1936, it bottomed out suddenly in the summer of 1937 and the nation went into a recession. At Roosevelt's request, Congress allocated nearly $4 billion for public works. Roosevelt's Farm Tenant Act, passed by Congress in 1937, made loans available to help farmers, but for most it was too late.

Along with many others across the nation during those dark days, the Crittendens looked for help from the federal government's Works Progress Administration. Large yellow government trucks came around regularly in the rural communities to distribute what were called "commodities"—foods with a long shelf life, such as flour, cornmeal, dried beans and peas, baking powder, salt, baking soda, lard, sugar, and canned foods. If it had not been for those commodities and the peanuts, the Crittendens would not have survived the winter. The trucks also distributed sweaters and coats. All the clothes looked alike, so everyone else knew where those clothes came from.

When one of her little classmates visited Helen after school that winter, she was surprised to see that the only thing Mrs. Crittenden served for their supper was one small can of potted meat and some crackers. His lack of nutrition affected Howie's health and his stamina to some degree and caused him to have serious problems with his teeth. Many times he played in basketball games for Cuba when he was not feeling well, but he never complained. Although his childhood circumstances weakened him in some ways, they also toughened him, teaching him to adjust to whatever deprivation befell him. He learned to do his best in spite of adversity.

12

The Migration

We are dropping down the ladder rung by rung:
And the measure of our torment is the measure of our youth.
God help us, for we knew the worst too young.
—Rudyard Kipling

In late spring of 1943, Willie Crittenden moved to Detroit to find work. His plan was to save enough money to send for Alta Ruth and the twins. Before he left, he moved his family from Pilot Oak into the house his oldest daughter Emily and her husband had just vacated in their own move to Detroit. Alta and the twins would live there until school was out, and then they would leave for the city.

This house was near the Kentucky-Tennessee border on KY 166. One side of the road was in Kentucky, the other in Tennessee. The house was situated in an isolated area, a little over a mile from Dukedom, a town well known for its criminal activities. It was not the ideal place for a woman with two small children and no transportation to live. Now that Willie was not sharecropping, they had neither mule nor wagon, items the landowner had provided.

To the twins' delight, Emily had left her pet, an old bulldog named Jiggs, for their protection. Jiggs had a fierce bark and plenty of experience chasing away the stragglers and drunks who occasionally wandered into the yard at night. He was also a boon companion for the twins and their beloved Collie. The other good thing about living in that house, aside from its being better built than their last one and rent free, was that their nearest neighbors were the Floyds, whose farm was a mile across the field. It was here that Howie and Doodle became friends, spending much of their time together in school and out.

After school each day, they would go to one or the other's home, help with chores, and then play. They sometimes chased each other for hours, running barefoot all over the fields. Other times they played basketball. Emily's husband had nailed an old basket to the side of the barn and had left his basketball for Howie. The boys played with that ball until it fell apart.

This was the year they got to see their high school varsity team play. Once or twice a week, their teacher would take all the boys in the class upstairs to the gymnasium to watch the varsity practice. On a couple of occasions they watched the team play an afternoon game. On some days the teacher turned the boys loose in the gym, giving them a rubber ball to play with. The ball had no air in it, so they could not dribble it. All they could do was run up and down the court, trying to get the ball away from whoever had it and then throwing it at the basket. Howie and Doodle usually managed to keep the ball to themselves while the other boys chased after them.

Willie got a job as janitor at Michigan Tool Company, and by late April had sent Alta Ruth an envelope stuffed with three bus tickets, two $20 bills, and a note saying he had rented an apartment and wanted her and the twins to come to Detroit. Not one to express emotions, he simply wrote that he missed them and wanted them to come soon.

Just as they were preparing to go, Howie came down with scarlet fever. In those days, scarlet fever, like polio and Spanish flu, was a dreaded disease. Once it was determined that a person had it, a quarantine sign had to be posted on the house where the infected person lived. No one inside the house was supposed to come out, and no one from the outside could go in. A loyal friend, Lexie Floyd brought Alta Ruth sacks of groceries from the commodity truck and set them on the steps of the house. She would wave to Alta and the twins as they smiled to her from the window. Fortunately, neither Helen nor her mother came down with the disease. After Howie recovered, Alta made arrangements for them to leave for Detroit.

Before daybreak one morning in May 1943, Lexie, James, and Doodle arrived in their horse-drawn wagon at the Crittenden's house to take the twins and their mother to the bus station in Fulton. For the twins, the saddest thing about their departure was learning that they had to leave Collie and Jiggs behind. Grief-stricken, Howie stared at his mother in disbelief. Helen pursed her lips and stubbornly refused to get into the wagon without her pets. Angrily, Alta Ruth snatched her up and plopped her down on the back seat of the wagon. For the full nine miles to the bus station, Helen sobbed fitfully, while Howie lay silently on his back staring at the dark morning sky. Years later, Howie would still see in his mind's eye his abandoned dogs as they looked that morning.

The Crittendens' new home in Detroit was a small four-room upstairs apartment, sparsely furnished, with no yard in which the twins could play. Alta Ruth was afraid to let them go outside, so the twins were confined to the cramped apartment. Living in the city required an adjustment that none of them could make. They had grown too accustomed to the freedom that farm life provided, and they were depressed even though they were reunited with their father and Emily and her husband. For weeks the twins came home from school crying every afternoon. The large school, the strict teachers, the crowded classrooms, the traffic in the halls, and the screeching sirens of the air-raid drills signaling the students to crawl under their desks were all far too much for the twins at first. Most damaging of all was their inability to keep up academically.

One day the teacher talked about the importance of good posture and announced that she would give a reward to the student who sat the straightest all that day. Howie saw the offer as an opportunity to succeed in at least one thing. That entire day, he sat, stood, and walked ramrod straight. He won the award along with his teacher's praise, and her praise meant more to him than she realized. If ever a child yearned for approval, it was Howie Crittenden, and he worked hard to deserve it. Soon he and Helen began to excel in reading and math lessons, and both improved their grammar and pronunciation. They no longer dreaded going to school.

After a year in Detroit, the Crittendens moved into another three-room apartment in a slightly better neighborhood. It was here that his mother received a telegram one winter afternoon in 1944 saying that W. A., a corporal in the army, was missing in action. A few weeks later, when another telegram announced W. A. had been taken prisoner by the Germans, she collapsed on the couch and sobbed for hours. She felt that the world she knew was falling apart. Although she was not told this at the time, W. A. had been captured by the Germans near Dijon, France, while serving in General George S. Patton's hard-driving U.S. Third Army. He barely survived that terrible winter in the prisoners' camp.

The twins transferred that year to another elementary school where physical education classes were required and where Howie had a chance to play basketball. When the other children and the instructor saw him shoot the ball with a two-handed set shot, their eyes widened. "Hey, where did you learn to shoot like that?" the teacher asked. "Howie, you've got a natural knack for handling the ball, and you move like lightning. You could be a great basketball

Whether playing basketball or checkers, Howie and Doodle were inseparable. Here they compete in a checker game at Harper's Store. (Photo courtesy of Charles Floyd.)

player some day." When she had the class shoot layups, Howie again had the satisfaction of doing better than any of the others.

The twins continued to do well in school. Helen was chosen to work on the yearbook, and Howie was chosen to be one of the safety guards, a position that made him feel proud—only students who had earned the teachers' trust were selected. By this time, Howie had a paper route and a secondhand bicycle with no fenders. Although he had to get up at 4:00 every morning to make his deliveries before school, he did not mind. He gave the money he earned to his mother to save for their return home to Kentucky.

Shortly before the war ended, a letter arrived saying that W. A. was among those soldiers released from a German prison camp and that he would be discharged with honors. He and his younger brother Norman, who was also in the army, would soon be back in the States and reunited with their family.

After school closed that summer of 1945, the Crittendens returned to Pilot Oak and moved into a four-room house, next door to Wagoner's store. In the front room of this house was a switchboard installed the previous year by some men who had created a battery-operated party-line telephone system for Pilot Oak. Instead of paying rent, the Crittendens agreed to operate the switchboard. This confining job fell to Alta Ruth, of course. No call could be made without going through that switchboard, and the lines ran all the way to Dukedom and to Fulton.

With the money he had saved by working in Detroit, Willie bought a thirty-acre farm, a mule, a mare, four cows, fifty chickens, three pigs, a plow, and a wagon, and some farm tools. Luckily for Howie again, this farm adjoined the Floyds' place.

Being back home and having Doodle to run and play basketball with made Howie happy. His return meant much more to Doodle, for it helped fill a void that had tragically occurred while the Crittendens were living in Detroit.

13

The Tragedy

By grief the soul is torn asunder.
—Proverbs 27:14

The most important person in Doodle's young life was his brother James, three years older. Doodle adored James, and James loved his little brother with all his heart. They worked and played together. As it always is, even with best friends, some bickering went on between them occasionally, but it always ended in laughter. Until James turned thirteen and Doodle ten in 1944, they were constant companions. But as soon as James reached his teenage years, he wanted time on his own to read or just be alone. He had outgrown most of the games that his younger brother still enjoyed playing. Loving him as he did, Doodle was puzzled by what he thought was rejection. Then, too, their mother had not only instructed but also extracted a solemn promise from him that he would always stay with James to see to it that he did not hurt himself when he had a seizure. James, you see, had epilepsy.

James Floyd looked like the archetypal American youth—a poster boy. Not only was he handsome, he was good natured, intelligent, and kind. (Photo courtesy of Charles Floyd.)

Tall, muscular, strong, and handsome, James weighed 175 pounds by the time he was thirteen. He had thick blond straight hair that he parted on the side and kept neatly cut and combed. He had a smooth olive complexion, denim-blue eyes, a square jaw line, and a resolute expression.

All through school he made straight A's, and he also saw to it that Doodle did well in his schoolwork. Unlike Doodle, James was an avid reader, and he won awards nearly every year for reading more library books than anyone else at the school. James read big books, too, books that the other children called hard; he did not just read the Zane Grey and Tarzan series. He was elected president of his class and also president of the Future Farmers of America, an organization that the school required all boys to join. James was much loved by his family, and also by his friends, teachers, and folks in Pilot Oak. Everyone who knew the Floyds knew that the family was immensely proud of James and had great expectations for him. They knew, too, that Vodie lived vicariously through the boy, for James was all that Vodie was not and yet wished to be.

Around the age of six or seven, James fell from a moving wagon and was knocked unconscious. After he awakened, he seemed all right. Were it not for a bad bruise on the side of his head, there would have been no sign that he had fallen. He continued to grow and develop normally, but when he was around eleven, he began having seizures. His first attack occurred one morning shortly after Christmas while his dad was working in Detroit. His mother was frightened, not knowing what to think or do. The old folks in Pilot Oak told her that children sometimes outgrow such "fits" and that nothing could be done but pray that James outgrew his. He was otherwise healthy and intelligent. He did not appear to suffer any adverse effects after having a seizure, so she did not take him to see Dr. Page.

What worried Lexie more than anything was the possibility that he might injure himself in a fall during one of these attacks. During the seizures he lost consciousness and fell to the floor. His arms and legs would jerk, he would perspire profusely, and then become rigid. His complexion would turn dusky or pale. Sometimes he bit the inside of his mouth and tongue, or hurt his arm or shoulder in the fall. The seizures lasted for only seconds or a few minutes; they often stopped almost as quickly as they started. But they always left him quite drowsy and exhausted. Sometimes he would sleep for hours after an attack.

Fearing that he would hit his head or choke or cut his tongue or break a bone, Lexie explained to Doodle how to take care of James and instructed him never—never ever—to leave James alone. "Pretend," she said, "that you are the big brother. You look after James."

The seizures were unpredictable, but James could sense they were coming on moments before they occurred. He would go for weeks without having one and then have ten to fifteen in one day. Coping with epilepsy was difficult for the child. It limited his freedom. Riding a bike could have been too dangerous if he were in the wrong place at the wrong time. He could not participate in some school or church activities for fear of creating a disruption. He could not go fishing or for walks alone. Having spells at school was painfully embarrassing. Whenever he had an attack at school, the principal would call Doodle out of his class to come stay with his brother until he recovered. Not many people in Pilot Oak ever saw James without seeing Doodle nearby.

When the brothers got off the school bus every afternoon at Wagoner's, they walked the three miles home. Once while crossing the little wooden bridge down from Martha Casey's house, James had a seizure. He fell down, jerking and rolling. Terrified that James would drown if he rolled over into the creek below, Doodle, who was only a first grader at that time, jumped on top of his brother's twisting body and lay holding him in place as best he could till the seizure ended. Although that seizure was brief, it was most frightening because they were on the bridge. James did not remember the incident, but Doodle never forgot it.

During the winter that James had his first seizures, no one told Vodie, who was working in Detroit. When he returned home in the spring and saw his son having a seizure, he was shocked, frightened, and angry that he had not been told. He took his son to Cuba to see Dr. Page, who suggested that they all go to a specialist in Mayfield the next day. The Mayfield physician prescribed a new medication—Dilantin, which had just been developed in 1938 as an antiepileptic agent and was working miracles for people with epilepsy. It was expensive, and it had to be monitored regularly by Dr. Page. James had to take it daily. "You cannot miss a dose! Unless I tell you to stop taking it, do not stop," the Mayfield physician firmly instructed the boy and his father.

Once the dosage was correctly adjusted for his age and weight, James stopped having seizures. Dilantin worked its miracle and gave the child the confidence and freedom to do things that he had never done without great fear, such as stand up before a group, perform in a play, speak or read aloud in class. He had a lovely tenor voice, but he had never joined the chorus. Dilantin permitted him to join and to enjoy performing.

August 5, 1944, was a blistering hot, humid day. After lunch, James and Doodle walked with their parents to Wagoner's store, where folks gathered to talk about war news and about whether Roosevelt, frail with ill health, ought to run for a fourth term. For most of that afternoon, as James, Doodle, and other boys played basketball in front of the store, their parents sipped icy-cold Orange Crushes and talked quietly with their friends about the war, about their sons in the service. Bill, the Floyds' son, was in the army serving in the Pacific, and they worried about him all the time, especially after hearing that U.S. troops had landed on Guam on July 21. Everyone was tense after learning that young Clyde Pickens, the husband of one of Lexie's cousins, had been killed in action and that the Crittendens' oldest son, W. A., had been captured by the Germans.

Around 4:00 that afternoon, the Floyd family headed home for supper. James and Doodle took off running ahead of their parents and arrived at home long before them. Doodle often had headaches and that afternoon, after playing in the hot sun, he was suffering from a terrible one that running home and the heat had made worse. Once he stepped into his front yard, instead of going into the house or around to the backyard as he usually did, he dropped to the ground and stretched out on his belly under the big shade tree. With his head resting on his hands and turned toward the house, he watched James go around to the backyard. The house was built high off the ground and did not have any shrubbery around it, so Doodle could see the yard behind the house. He watched James's legs going toward the outhouse, and then he closed his eyes and tried to nap. A few seconds later, he opened them again and watched for James to come out.

Maybe twenty minutes or more passed before his parents walked past him and went straight into the house without saying a word to him. Then Doodle saw his dad looking out the window at him. Next he heard the back door open and slam shut. Through narrow slits of his eyes, he watched his father's legs go from the house toward the outhouse.

Suddenly he heard his father scream, and then yell to him to get Dr. Page and to hurry—to run. Filled with terror, Doodle broke out running across the pasture two miles to their nearest neighbor's house. Breathless, with tears staining his face and his heart pounding, he shouted to his nearly deaf elderly neighbor Ed Rhodes, whom he woke from a nap, that James needed help and that he needed it immediately. He cried, "Please, Mr. Rhodes, hurry, get Dr. Page! James is hurt bad! " The old man grabbed his hat, pulled up his suspenders, and jumped into his Model A. He spun out of his driveway, kicking up dust that settled on Doodle's sweaty face and arms.

Back at his house, Doodle saw his father sitting on the ground, cradling James in his arms, rocking him back and forth, crying helplessly. His mother was kneeling near him. She was sobbing into her apron, which she had pulled up around her face and was holding with the palms of both hands. James was dead. He had had a seizure in the outhouse and had fallen, striking his head against the door. When Dr. Page arrived, he said an artery in James's neck had ruptured and that nothing could be done. The child had drowned in his own blood.

Later, a young girl in Pilot Oak revealed to the family that James had said someone had told him that he did not need that expensive medicine and ought to stop wasting his folks' money.

The deeply saddened Floyd family gather at the cemetery after James was buried. Pictured left to right are Doodle's dad, Vodie; his mother, Lexie; his older brothers Hobert and Herschel; and his sister Lillian. Doodle is in front. (Photo courtesy of Charles Floyd.)

This person recommended that he take some kind of tea made from ground-up wild plant leaves instead, saying that it would do just as well as anything store-bought and save his parents' money. It is not known if James took her advice. But it is most likely that he did not.

The morning of the day he died, James told his mother that he and Doodle had been hiding money they had earned doing chores for some older people in Pilot Oak. They had buried their little sacks of change between the roots of the old tree in the front yard. With eerie prescience, he also told her that if anything ever happened to him, he wanted her to get his sack, which had almost $17 in it, and buy herself a gold ring. Vodie had never bought her a real wedding band, and she had always admired the wide gold ones in the *Sears, Roebuck & Co. Catalogue.* With great sadness, Lexie regretted not paying enough attention to what her son was telling her that morning. He often talked about doing things to make her life a little better. "That was just his way," she whispered to others.

James was laid to rest alongside the grave of his older brother Harold in the old Pinson graveyard, near First Baptist Church in Pilot Oak. His death had a profound effect on his family. James had been their special child. Vodie became even more of a loner—moody and melancholy. A tragic figure, he submerged himself in work, staying in the field far into the night. When he did come in for meals, he ate silently and then sat in his rocking chair with his eyes closed, never talking to anyone unless he had to. He made it clear, too, that he did not want to be spoken to. For over a year, he never turned on the radio. With Lillian and all the other boys except Doodle gone, the house was quiet. Lexie went about her duties listlessly. No longer did she hum or sing softly to herself while she worked.

Doodle, only eleven years old, was left alone much of the time to fend for himself. Not much attention was paid anymore to his coming and going. Yet his sorrow may have been the most profound of all, for he could not escape thinking that he was responsible for the accident. Had he followed James that day to the backyard, he could have saved him, he thought. His parents never suggested that they thought Doodle could have prevented James's accident, and no one in Pilot Oak or Cuba either said this or appeared to think it. But Doodle thought it. And his grief ran deep.

14

Mischief Makers

A wise man makes his father glad,
but a foolish son is a grief to his mother.
—Proverbs 10:1

Around the age of thirteen, Howie and Doodle got to thinking that they were grown up. Doodle, especially, started thinking of himself as a big guy—chewing on a cigar, spitting tobacco, comparing the budding bodices of female peers, and expanding his colorful vocabulary—all of which got him into varying degrees of trouble with his parents. One afternoon when his mother overheard him cursing, she washed his mouth out with a piece of her lye soap and asked him, "Charles, now how tasty are your words?"

In those days it was nearly impossible for any child to get away with any kind of wrongdoing. The folks in Pilot Oak, like the ones in Cuba, looked after each other's children, and they all expected the children to act right. Some mothers worked in Mayfield at the Merit Clothing Company and did not get home in the evenings until 5:30 or 6:00, about the same time their husbands came in from the fields, and much later than their children returned home from school. Others, like Lexie Floyd, lived far out in the country and could not possibly know what their children were doing all the time when they were away from home. But parents did not worry because every adult had authority to correct any child's behavior. Although the children were free to wander about, they were always being seen by someone from a kitchen window, back porch swing, garden, or field.

One beautiful warm afternoon when Doodle should have been in school but was playing basketball instead with three drop-outs in front of Harper's, he suddenly stopped in his tracks and listened intently. He thought he heard his dad's old Model A off in the distance. With so few automobiles in southern Graves County, just about anyone with a keen ear, like Doodle, could recognize the distinctive sound of each car. With his head cocked to one side, he stood still for a minute looking down the road, shading his eyes with his hand, squinting hard to see as far as he could. He reassured himself he had nothing to worry about, that his father would be in the field working at that time of day. Then, in the distance, he saw an old Ford stirring up a cloud of dust, barreling down the road toward Cuba at its top speed—twenty-five miles an hour. Doodle's heart pounded; he stiffened with dread.

Joe McPherson, the young assistant coach and history teacher, was not as lenient as some other Pilot Oak teachers. He reported Doodle's numerous absences to his parents. Vodie did not take the news lightly. A no-nonsense, hardworking man, Vodie could not tolerate "idleness" or "foolishness" in any of his children, and much to his dismay, his youngest child seemed to be too much inclined to both vices.

When Vodie saw his son standing in front of the store holding a basketball at 1:00 in the afternoon on a school day, he was furious. He brought his old car to an abrupt stop, leaned over to the passenger side, popped the door open with his huge hand, and yelled to Doodle, "Get in this car!" Then he gunned the motor, wrenched the wheel hard in the opposite direction, sped around a curve, swung into the school yard, and came to a screeching halt. Hearing the clatter, teachers and students ran to the windows. Right there—in front of the whole school, Vodie jumped out of the car, dragging Doodle out with him. He pulled a leather belt from his overalls pocket and gave his son three or four sound wops on the rear end with it. It was a most humiliating experience for Doodle, who went on to fail the sixth grade anyway. He said he failed on purpose, so that he and Howie could be in the same grade.

Doodle and Howie got into big trouble one day when they decided to trade one of Mrs. Crittenden's chickens for some cold drinks, candy, and comic books at the store. They figured old Mr. Wagoner would not pay attention; he was always drowsy in the afternoons, and they could pull their scheme off with ease. So while Doodle swiped the chicken from the Crittendens' backyard, adjacent to the store, Howie kept an eye on his mother in the house by peeping in the windows. The trade went smoothly with Mr. Wagoner, who pitched the chicken into his coop behind the store. Enjoying their refreshments, the boys had a great time, lying in the shade of the nearby plum tree. After a while Doodle sneaked the chicken from Mr. Wagoner's coop and placed it back into Mrs. Crittenden's yard. All was well—or so they thought. Little did they know that they had been under surveillance the whole time by an old lady living in the house behind the store. Informed, their mothers were ready for them when they got home—Howie and Doodle each got a whipping and a lecture that neither of them ever forgot. For atonement, they not only had to apologize to the storekeeper, but for the remainder of the summer they had to sweep his store daily and keep the saplings away from his fencerow.

That year, the one person who saved Doodle from quitting

school, running away from home, and doing heaven knows what else was Kindred Winston, the coach and principal at the Cuba School. Mr. Winston knew that James's death had been hard on the child and on his parents. He figured that the boy needed attention he was not getting from his parents, who were good people but grief-stricken. He knew Doodle was capable of becoming a good student and a good athlete, for the boy was intelligent and had a remarkable natural ability for basketball. Mr. Winston made a point of speaking to him every time he saw him, giving him a bit of encouragement on each occasion. He knew that keeping a troubled youngster such as Doodle involved in sports was the only way to keep him in school. After watching the boy on the basketball court, he would always say something like, "Say, Doodle, I sure like your steady control of the ball" or "By next year you'll make a great center and a great rebounder on the team. The way you keep moving while holding your arms wide open and elbows up is great! Man, you've got the touch!" One day he told Doodle, "Hey, you keep on doing what you're doing, and you'll be a great basketball star someday."

Eager to please Mr. Winston, Doodle did his schoolwork more attentively, and he stopped skipping class. At the end of that school year, he was surprised and sad to learn that Mr. Winston was leaving Cuba to become principal of a high school in South Fulton, Tennessee. Doodle thought he was at loose ends again. Without a coach, the school would be without a basketball team. Without a basketball team, what would be the point in going to school?

15

Jack Story

In the long run, men hit only what they aim at.
—Henry David Thoreau

In the fall of 1947, the people in Cuba were thrilled to have Jack Story at their school again. When coaching there once before, during 1942–1943, he had brought the team closer than it had ever been to the state tournament. He led Cuba to the district runner-up position, losing by only 1 point to Benton. Both teams went on to the 1943 regional tournament, where Cuba bowed out to Benton again.

A tall man, broad shouldered and slightly paunchy, Jack Story had a round face and soft, wavy brown hair that he kept short and combed straight back without a part. He was an intense man, not a glad-hander or backslapper, nor one to smile quickly either. He was direct and brief, and he meant just what he said. He never argued or cajoled. The people who knew him well said he appreciated good jokes, though he never told any; that he loved to eat lobster and enjoyed a drink now and then.

As coach, principal, and teacher, he was respected and admired even though he was a stern authority figure—whom no one questioned. He emphasized winning in academics and in sports, and he hated losing at anything. He had a little paper tacked on a wall in his office with a quote from Adolph Rupp on it: "If you think losing with good sportsmanship is as good as winning, then why in the hell do they keep score?"

In practice sessions, he would tell the boys, "Play to win!" His dark brown eyes could blaze with such intensity that his ballplayers, on many occasions, wished they could make themselves disappear. Except for perhaps two times during the five years he was with them, he never complimented them. He was a stickler for details. To a fearful student stammering, "But Coach, I'm . . . I'm . . . I'm trying," his usual response was "I do not want you to try, son. I want you to do it!"

As a bench coach, he was a model of stoic control, never shouting to players or leaping up to berate them or officials. He thought coaches who lost control of themselves were bad influences on their players. He would walk around the half-court during warm-ups and talk to the boys individually, putting each one on guard, telling him to be alert, what to look for, and saying such things as "Now, Doodle, you have not played against a guy like this Jerry Bird [from Corbin]. You're going to learn something tonight. Pay attention." Or he would say, "Doodle, stop watching him play! You play!"

His mother, Lillian Bernice Emerson, was only seventeen when Jack was born on April 30, 1917, in the southernmost part of Calloway County in a little place called Hazel. Lillian wanted to name her son John Boyd Story, but her husband, Leslie Abraham "L. A." Story, ten years older than she, insisted on naming the child Jack. A compromise of sorts was reached, and the infant was christened simply J. B., but called Jack.

His parents knew the value of education, and each one earned

Jack Story at three years of age. (Photo courtesy of Barbara Story Crowell.)

a master of arts degree in a time when most people left school after the seventh or eighth grade. In fact, Lillian received two graduate degrees, one from Murray State Teachers College and another from Wayne State University in Detroit. L. A. Story taught in several area schools before becoming principal at the Pilot Oak School late in his career, so Jack attended several schools before he graduated from Almo, a high school in Calloway County.

Although he did not play basketball as a child, Jack was always interested in the game. He played basketball at Almo but only as a substitute. His coach, James "Baby" DeWeese, became superintendent of Graves County schools and Jack's employer. Later, Jack would tell his players, "Always be honest and fair in dealing with everyone you meet because you never know who will be your boss or your father-in-law someday."

Excellent at mathematics and science, Jack graduated from Almo when he was only sixteen. Knowing that he wanted to coach basketball, he went straight to Murray State Teachers College in Murray, Kentucky, where he majored in physical education and math. Although he participated in boxing, basketball, and football at Murray, he never starred in any of the sports.

By his junior year, he ran out of tuition money and had to withdraw from college to find a job. In 1936 teachers were not required to have a college degree, and Jack took the first job offered to him—coaching at Fairbanks, a tiny community in Graves County four miles from the Tennessee state line. The Fairbanks School had one teacher for all the lower grades, two teachers for the high school, and a total enrollment of thirty students. It had no gymnasium, just a dirt court behind the school, and no basketball team.

Only ten boys were enrolled in the high school, and one of them was a Pentecostal who believed he would suffer eternal damnation if he played sports. In order to make a basketball team, Jack pulled a boy from the eighth grade. Next, he nailed a basketball goal up in one of the large rooms upstairs and had the boys practice shooting baskets. As often as he could, he took them to the school in Sedalia, a little settlement nearby, where they practiced in the indoor gymnasium. He had them practice shooting baskets for hours sometimes, telling them the point of the game is to score and to keep their opponents from scoring. And score his team did.

In his first year coaching basketball at Fairbanks, Jack performed what was considered by many to be a coaching miracle. He guided his team to winning the district tournament—the first and the only such win in the history of that little school. The championship game was played in the old American Legion building in Mayfield. Fairbanks' smashing victory over the large urban high school team sent the Mayfield fans reeling in despair over what they believed was a humiliating defeat. Only nineteen years old at the time, Jack was younger than a couple of boys on the team; the age limit for high school players was twenty. Despite his youth, he had an uncanny ability to command respect. The boys appreciated his recognition of their individual strengths.

While he was coaching at Fairbanks, his father was principal of the school at Pilot Oak, which had an excellent basketball team called the War Horses. Those boys earned their way to Pilot Oak's first Kentucky State Tournament in 1937. Jack gladly accepted his dad's invitation to go along with him and the team to handle the money and to act as team manager. In the opening round of that 1937 tournament, Pilot Oak beat Breckenridge Training of Morehouse 30-27, but bowed out in the quarterfinals to Midway 32-23. Midway went on to win the championship. That state tournament left such an indelible impression on Jack that he never missed attending another, except the year he spent in the navy.

As he sat in Alumni Gym in Lexington that night in 1937, enthralled by the closing ceremony in which Midway received the magnificent championship trophy, Jack told the Pilot Oak boys sitting next to him, "I'm going to come back here someday and win me one of those!"

Soon after he arrived at Fairbanks, he fell in love with Mary Lee Pittman, a student at the high school. After a brief courtship, they slipped away on June 14, 1936, to Paris, Tennessee, where they were married by a justice of the peace. They married without their parents' consent or knowledge. Afraid to break the news to their families—especially to Mary's—each continued to live for a few weeks as they had before—Mary Lee at home, and Jack in his rented room. But once told, their parents gave the young couple their blessings.

After Mary Lee graduated from high school in May 1937, she and Jack moved into a modest apartment in Murray so that he could finish work on his degree. Both got part-time jobs; she as a waitress and he as an assistant to an electrician. On August 24, 1938, the first of their three children, Rex Daniel Story, was born.

Jack earned his bachelor's degree in 1939 and immediately went to work coaching at Centertown in Ohio County. After their second child, Carolyn, was born in 1940, he found it difficult to support his family on his meager salary. With two small children, Mary Lee was unable to continue working outside the home. Jack loved his job, but the salaries for teachers and coaches were pitifully low. Even following a tight budget, they could not make ends meet.

The rural areas of the Jackson Purchase did not have electric power in the early 1940s, so there were no industries to provide jobs. Many young people migrated to the industrialized North, hoping to find better lives. Howie's and Doodle's older siblings and their fathers had done just that. With its big automotive plants and factories, Detroit provided work that was not available elsewhere. So, like many other poor people in the late 1930s and 1940s, Jack moved his family to Detroit in 1941, planning to work there long enough to save money to buy a reliable used automobile and a home back in Kentucky. Once they returned to Graves County, they figured that

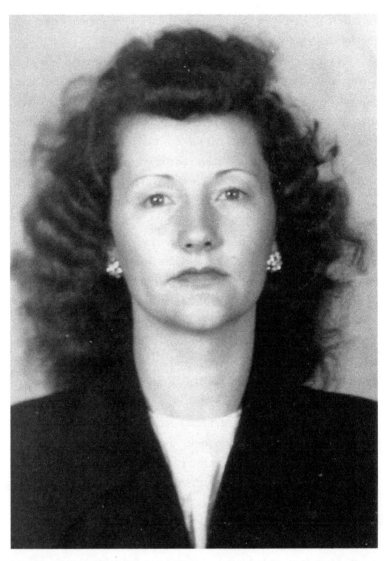

Mary Lee Story operated the concession stand at the school, the proceeds from which paid for basketball equipment. She and the children traveled with Coach Story to away games, where she also kept statistical charts. (Photo courtesy of Barbara Story Crowell.)

Jack could go back to coaching basketball and Mary Lee could stay home with the children. But only a few months of living in the city, with its dirty, loud, crowded streets, and of working in a factory as a tool and die maker convinced Jack that he and his family needed to go back home to Kentucky as quickly as they could.

On December 7, 1941, the United States declared war on Japan and then four days later on Germany and Italy. Jack expected to be called into the military at any time, and he did not want to leave Mary Lee and the children in Detroit. In 1942 he moved his family back to western Kentucky, where economic conditions were just beginning to improve, thanks to the efforts of Graves County native Alben Barkley, then serving in the U.S. Senate.

As the Senate majority leader from 1937 to 1947, Barkley had extraordinary control of domestic affairs while President Franklin Delano Roosevelt focused his attention on the war and foreign affairs. Remembering the isolation and poverty of his own childhood in Graves County, Barkley fought to get improvements and electric power in all rural areas across the nation, and especially in western Kentucky. He was instrumental in getting the high dams built on the Tennessee River and later on the Cumberland.

In building those dams, the Tennessee Valley Authority provided many jobs for Purchase people like Jack Story. He immediately went to work as a master electrician at the Shawnee Steam Plant after he returned to Mayfield in 1942. The tourist business that gradually grew around the land between Kentucky and Barkley lakes also provided employment, as did the two defense plants that Barkley had the federal government build in the Purchase in 1941 and 1942.

One of these plants was at Viola, thirty miles outside of Mayfield. Also at Barkley's urging, the Pennsylvania Salt Manufacturing Company was the first private industry to build a huge plant on the Tennessee River near Calvert City. It soon became evident that Jackson Purchase people had been agrarians for so long that they found

Left to right: Rex Story, Caroline Story, and Barbara Story. (Photo courtesy of Barbara Story Crowell.)

it difficult to become industrialized. They resented the formalized management of unions and wanted to run the plants their own way.

Upon their return to Mayfield, the Storys found that the war had changed life in Graves County dramatically. Nearly all of the young men had left for the armed services, and many older men had moved north to work in defense plants. Women who had never worked outside their homes were working now in the Mayfield clothing factories—the Merit, the Curlee, and the Andover—or at the new ammunition plant at nearby Viola. Some of the older men worked at the defense plant too.

The Storys rented an apartment in Mayfield. With the help of a neighbor lady who agreed to tend to the children, Mary Lee went to work full-time as a presser at the Merit Clothing factory. Although their life together was still uncertain, it was, for the time being, more financially secure than it had ever been. In 1942, when Jack was asked to coach at the Cuba School, he was reluctant to give up his well-paying job as master electrician, but the thought of coaching basketball again pulled at his heart so strongly that he could not refuse.

The first of December 1942, he started at the Cuba School. By early 1943, the draft was including teachers and married men with children. Expecting to receive his call into the service at any moment, Jack left Cuba at the end of the 1943 school year and went to work for the Tennessee Valley Authority for over a year before entering the navy. Their third child, Barbara, was born on January 7, 1945, before he went to boot camp and school in Biloxi, Mississippi. He ended up serving only a short stint before the war ended in the summer of 1945. After mustering out of the service, he worked briefly in St. Louis before returning to Mayfield and his job as an electrician for the Shawnee Steam Plant. In 1947, after he learned that Kindred Winston was leaving the Cuba School, Jack applied for Winston's job and got it.

Jack and Mary Lee Story in 1945 while he was serving in the navy during World War II. (Photo courtesy of Barbara Story Crowell.)

With three small children now, Jack and Mary Lee knew he needed to continue working part-time at the Shawnee plant, and so he signed on for third shift for three or four nights a week. Such a schedule allowed him to work at school all day until late afternoon, or even much later when he had ball games. After completing his school day, he would drive the ten miles home to Mayfield, get a couple of hours of sleep and a bite to eat, and then drive thirty miles to the plant, where he worked until the early morning hours. Many a morning, he drove straight from the plant to the school without a chance to rest, eat, change clothes, or see his family. His schedule would have been fatal for someone who needed more than three or four hours of sleep each night, but he seemed to settle into his demanding routine that fall of 1947 without too much trouble.

Jack Story looked after the children in his school and identified those who needed special help. For a while he went out of his way each morning to pick up a boy who lived so far out that the school bus did not pass anywhere near his house. He saw to it that every child got a good hot lunch whether that child could pay for it or not. The school furnished nourishing meals, too, with foods raised on nearby farms and prepared by good cooks.

When twelve-year-old Corky Hill lost his left arm in a hunting accident in the early fall of 1950, Coach Story noticed that the boy's grades were slipping and that he was keeping to himself on the playground and in the lunchroom. During the lunch recess, he would sit alone in the gym watching the others shoot baskets. One day Coach Story told Doodle to throw the ball to Corky and have him shoot from the sideline a few times. Not long after that, he invited him to come out for the basketball team, but at first Corky refused. Finally he agreed because Coach Story had convinced him that he had to try to do things, and that he could learn to do anything he wanted to do if only he tried. After Coach Story realized Corky did not want to wear the sleeveless uniform, he let him practice in blue jeans and a T-shirt.

On the night of the junior varsity's first game, Coach Story told Corky that he would have to wear a uniform, and the boy agreed to do so. Coach Story put him in the game, and to the crowd's surprise he scored. Right after that game, Corky said he'd decided that he was not going to let the loss of his arm change his life, but just change the way he had to do things. Much later on he said he did not know what would have happened to him if it had not been for Jack Story.

Some mornings the coach would stop at one of the stores to talk with the men who gathered there. He would have a glass of milk; he never drank coffee, believing it was unhealthy. Those visits always included talks about whatever was happening on the local and national scenes and ended with what was going on with the neighboring coaches, or with the Wildcats, or with Diddle's Hilltoppers at Western. Jack would leave in time to be at school when the buses arrived. He taught civics and math classes in the morning; in the afternoon he coached the varsity basketball team and taught physical education. His days were full.

16

Sowing the Seeds

The very essence of leadership is that you have to have a vision.
You can't blow an uncertain trumpet.
—Theodore Hesburgh

One afternoon in the fall of 1947, shortly after Jack Story started work at the Cuba School, he was in his office waiting for the lunch recess to end. It was a typical early October day, still too warm to wear a jacket. The windows were open wide, and the noise from the playground drifted into the room.

A few minutes before the bell was to ring, Jack shoved the papers that he had been reading aside and walked from his desk to the window and looked out onto the playground. Some little girls were sitting under the shade of the big oak tree with their lunch boxes scattered about on the ground while others were taking turns pushing on swings made from old tires attached to ropes tied to a large branch of the tree. Another group was playing pop the rope.

Off to one side on a pounded-dirt court, five skinny, shaggy-haired boys dressed in overalls and plow shoes were playing basketball. Their spirited improvisations captured Jack Story's attention. The tallest one of the five had astonishing natural ability to fake his passes to the smallest boy, who moved so fast as he dribbled the ball that he seemed to be floating above the ground. The tall one faking passes did so in such a comical manner that the others were bent over laughing. The stocky-built kid could block and screen, while another boy, a shorter, feisty, sandy-haired fellow, had an unusual ability to jump with either foot and shoot baskets. When the good-looking boy with the dark curly hair got the chance, he shot with surprising accuracy from all over. All five boys handled the ball, shot, and moved with natural ease. In a happy mood, Jack Story went home that evening and informed his wife that he had finally found a championship team that day and in a most unlikely place— the eighth grade.

A few days later after lunch recess, instead of meeting with his varsity, Jack met with the five eighth-grade boys he had watched on the playground. Making them feel grown-up, he shook hands with each one as they told him their names: the comic one who faked passes so well was Charles Kenneth Floyd, nicknamed "Doodle"; the small boy who dribbled the ball well was Howard Crittenden, called "Howie"; the curly-haired shooter was Jimmie Webb; the stocky blocker, Raymon McClure; and the feisty jumper, Joe Buddy Warren. Grabbing his straw hat from the hook on the wall, Coach Story led them outside of the lunchroom, asking, "Say, I've been wondering if you all are interested in making up a basketball team?" They looked at him quizzically, shrugged their shoulders, and grinned. Delighted that the coach was paying this kind of attention to them, they followed him out to the old oak tree in the schoolyard, where he suggested they sit down in the shade and talk a while.

A large man, Jack Story looked awkward as he bent down to sit on the ground. He leaned back against the tree with his heavy legs crossed at the ankles, loosened his tie, and unbuttoned his collar. Howie and Doodle clamored to sit on either side of him. As if he were speaking to much older boys, Jack began talking about basketball, about what it means to be a team, about what it means to compete and to win.

He talked about what he called the "grandest sports event in the world"—the Kentucky Boys High School Basketball Tournament, about how it was started in Danville in 1916 and later moved to Louisville and then to Lexington. He said that right from the start the monopoly on the title had been held by the big city schools—like Louisville Manual, which had an enrollment of perhaps three thousand, or Lexington Lafayette with twenty-five hundred. He named other schools the boys had never heard of—Louisville Male, Saint Xavier, Owensboro High, Henry Clay, and Ashland Paul Blazer. He explained that in all those years of tournaments, less than a handful of teams from unknown little places like theirs, with high schools that had fewer than a hundred students enrolled, had ever won the championship. But when those little places did win, their victories were so much sweeter. Then he shocked them by saying that *they* could win the state tournament by the time they were seniors—that is, he added, if they wanted to and if they started right then preparing themselves to win.

Fascinated by all they had heard him say, they still did not quite understand what he was telling them. They had never played on a team, and no one had ever talked to them the way he was talking to them about playing basketball. They did not even know the rules of the game, and here this grown man—this coach, their principal—was telling them *they* could win the state championship when they got to be seniors. Why, they had never even thought about being seniors, much less winning anything. What little they knew about basketball they had learned from watching their older brothers or other boys play, mostly in front of the stores. Except for a few occasions when their grammar school teachers had let them watch the varsity team practice or play games at school, they had not seen other teams play.

All they realized that afternoon was that Coach Story loved basketball, and that he knew everything there was to know about it. He explained how the state was divided into many districts, and how the teams were placed in the districts. He could name every team that had ever played in the state tournament and what regionals they had won, who their coaches were, and who had scored what, how, and why. He knew all about the Wildcats and the Hilltoppers, too. He had studied basketball on the national scale as well. He fascinated them with his talk and with the attention he was giving them.

The next afternoon Coach Story talked to the boys again. This time he fell into a storytelling mode, talking about the time years ago, before any of the boys were born, when little Carr Creek faced the mighty Ashland. Clear across Kentucky, on the opposite end of the state from us, he told them, in the far southeastern corner in the Appalachian region of Knott County, an unknown little school called Carr Creek made basketball history in 1928. It was the first little school to work its way to the state tournament—an astonishing feat, for Carr Creek had a total enrollment of forty-one students: twenty-three girls and eighteen boys. It had no gymnasium, trained coach, or uniforms, and no transportation either, except horses and mules.

The starters were all kin to each other. Two were brothers and cousins to the other three. They had grown up playing basketball together and had played in all kinds of weather, usually on a dirt court on the side of a hill near the school. Many times the ground was so muddy they could not dribble the ball. They walked or rode horseback miles to play in games in their area. But, he emphasized, all the things they did not have were offset by what they did have. Then, raising his left hand, Coach Story struck each finger as he enumerated Carr Creek's strengths: a natural ability that they had worked hard to develop, a love for the game, a willingness to work together, and an understanding of what it means to be on a team. Most important, he pointed out, was their strong will to win and their strong community support.

Far too modest about his role, Oscar Morgan, their coach, used to laugh and say that he did not have to do much coaching, just make the arrangements to play the games and chaperone. Coach Story explained that Morgan and his Mountaineers were the first to use the man-to-man full-court press that is so commonly used now.

Coach Story went on to explain that in 1928, Kentucky's teams were separated into A and B categories, with the winner of each category meeting to compete for the state trophy. Carr Creek won the B championship by beating Lawrenceburg High, 37-11. Ashland won the A championship. When that happened, every basketball fan in the state wanted to see these two teams—David and Goliath—play each other. That game attracted the largest crowd that had ever seen a high school game in Kentucky up to that time, and many hundreds were turned away.

Ashland was one of the largest schools in eastern Kentucky, and it was heavily favored when it met Carr Creek in the championship game. Yet Ashland struggled with Carr Creek's almost flawless man-to-man defense. The game went into four overtime periods, with Ashland making two more free throws than Carr Creek and barely winning, 13-11. The newspapers reporting the game called attention to the fact that Carr Creek had played straight through the district and the regional tournaments without calling a time-out and without committing a single personal foul. "Now that," said Coach Story, "is playing real basketball!"

The score was so low, he explained, because of "stalling" or "freezing" the ball—a tactic used to protect a lead, and one he wanted them to learn. When a team got a few points ahead, it would do its best to hold onto the ball by passing and faking plays, or both, unless a player had an irresistibly good shot or a free throw. No time limit was set on how long a team could hold the ball by passing or by dribbling it. They could keep it until the clock ran out. For the teams with excellent dribblers and passers, this method provided an ideal way to keep the other side from scoring. Once a team got ahead in the last quarter, it would play keep-away with the ball. If a player in possession of the ball was fouled during this time, he had a choice: he could take the free throw or he could keep possession by taking the ball out of bounds. Then he could run the clock out so that the opposing team would not have a chance to score. After watching fourteen-year-old Howie handle the ball artfully without any training whatsoever, Coach Story knew that he had a player who could develop into a dribbler capable of using this stalling strategy to his team's advantage.

Although Carr Creek did not win that championship, Coach Story said, the team's players put up a real fight. They were outstanding enough to get invited to go with Ashland to Chicago to participate in the 1928 National Invitational High School Basketball Tournament, held annually after the state tournaments. For a while it looked as if the two Kentucky teams would play each other again in the national finals. But after winning three games, Carr Creek lost to a team from Georgia, a team that Ashland beat in the final game. So Ashland won the national title, too. But Carr Creek got just as much, if not more, national publicity. Coach Story was showing the boys that the size of the school has nothing necessarily to do with the winning. It is how determined a team is to win that makes the difference. Carr Creek exemplified the kind of determination that Story wanted to inspire in his boys.

The one element of high school basketball that Jack Story never once talked to his boys about was what were then called "colored" basketball teams, even though two such teams were nearby:

one, Dunbar High, only ten miles away in Mayfield and the other, Lincoln High, thirty-four miles away in Paducah. In the late 1940s, when Coach Story was teaching his team the history of basketball and inspiring his players to earn their way to the state tournament and win it, Kentucky, like much of the nation, was separated into two worlds—one for whites and the other for blacks.

No black people lived in the Pilot Oak or Cuba area when the Cubs were growing up, so the Cubs did not know any until they went away to college. In those days of Jim Crow laws, there were few black farmers; most black people lived in towns and cities. It was not until after the 1954 U.S. Supreme Court decision *Brown v. Board of Education* that segregation laws very slowly began to disappear, and not until 1957 that the first black team, Lexington Dunbar High, was permitted to join the Kentucky High School Athletic Association.

Had it not been for those cruel segregation laws, several black teams, including Horse Cave, Louisville Central, and Lexington Dunbar, would have challenged the Cubs.

17

Preparing to Win

It's not enough to dream about winning; you have to prepare
yourselves to win. You have to work hard to make it happen!
—Coach Jack Story

All coaches have their own methods of motivating their players.
They have favorite words they emphasize, and Coach Story's was
determination. He applied it to every human endeavor, believing that
nobody ever achieves anything worthwhile unless he is determined
to do so and has prepared himself for the challenge. He warned the
boys, "Nobody's going to give you anything. Don't be thinking they
are. It's not enough to dream about winning, you have to prepare
yourselves to win. You will have to work hard. You see, what some
call 'good luck' is nothing but the result of hard work."

He loved seeing in them a strong spirit of competition, and he
did all he could to encourage that spirit. He indelibly impressed the
idea in their minds that while it is nice to win the regional, it is absolutely divine to win the state basketball tournament. He described
all the wonderful things that happened to a team after it had won

the championship. Before they left him that afternoon, the boys were sold on the idea that yes, they would bring that honor home to Cuba in 1952 when they were seniors. From that day on, they shared Jack Story's dream.

Although they knew Coach Story was passionate about basketball, they did not realize he was obsessed with the idea of coaching a championship team. At night after his wife and children had gone to sleep, he would sit at his kitchen table going over and over the stats. He would think about the next day's practice sessions or the last game his team had played and try to figure out why mistakes were made.

He read all the books and magazines about basketball that he could lay his hands on and pored over the sports pages in the daily newspapers. Whenever he had the time to do so, he scouted games, spotted players, learned new techniques, and always kept shot charts. When he could not go to watch a team that he was interested in, he would send someone to go for him and keep charts. One of the Cubs' classmates, Donald Poyner, sometimes did this job for him.

On many cold nights, Mary Lee would wrap their small children up warmly, and they would all go with Jack in the old Plymouth to some basketball game as far as thirty or forty miles away. She never complained; it would not have changed anything anyway. She knew early on that if she wanted to stay married to him, she would have to live with basketball too. Devoted to him and their children, she conformed to his schedule and wishes. He taught her and later the children how to keep records for him, and they did so for years. He acquired basketball films from college coaches' libraries and watched them over and over. He closely followed the progress of his colleagues in other high schools and of his idols—Rupp and Diddle—who were then earning their immortality coaching basketball.

Malleable and eager to learn and to please, the eighth-grade

Even as a toddler Donald Poyner was seeing eye to eye with his dad, E. B. Poyner, who went on to become Cuba's official basketball ticket agent at the Cubs' home games. Donald became class president and valedictorian. He tutored a number of the players in their schoolwork. (Photo courtesy of Donald Poyner.)

boys provided Jack Story with all the raw material he needed for a championship team. His determination to mold them into athletes soon became evident to all the teachers. Every day after lunch, he talked to the boys for a while and then put them to work learning the fundamentals of the game. As long as the weather permitted, they practiced outside while the varsity used the gym.

He demanded that each player have a thorough knowledge of the basic rules and plays of the game. He would say that it was good to be able to do some fancy passing and dribbling but only if you thoroughly knew the fundamentals. You cannot win a game with showboating. His mantra was Practice! Practice! Practice! Score! Score! Score!

Jack Story was ahead of his time in some of his coaching techniques. Unlike other coaches, he did not have the players on the floor during practice all learning the same technique at the same time. He encouraged them to experiment, to perfect their natural abilities to jump, shoot, dribble, and guard. Although each boy was allowed to try out for the position he felt most comfortable playing, each had to learn the basic moves of all the other positions as well.

Howie and Joe Buddy were short and fast and were inclined to run the court, dribble, and shoot. They were natural guards. Doodle, the tallest among them at six feet four, was an ideal pivot, center, passer, and shooter. Jimmie, who was nearly as tall as Doodle, was a natural forward who knew how to keep the ball high at shoulder level and to move fast. He could rebound and score remarkably well. Stocky and wide, Raymon was a born rebounder and blocker. In many practice sessions, Coach Story had them each play different roles.

He was silent about their flashy moves and behind-the-back passes that did not always connect. He did not mind their trying out unusual shot-making techniques or their failed attempts. Unlike other coaches, he let them ad lib on the court at times. When he saw they were getting too tense in practice, he would have them stop practicing for three days. He never wanted them to lose their creativity or their love for playing the game.

Following the coach's instructions, Howie developed into an extraordinary "keep-away" dribbler who could maintain possession of the ball for several minutes at a time. Doodle's weird winding windmill shots contradicted the tried-and-true methods of shooting. Perhaps if some other coach had seen Doodle, as an eighth grader, getting ready to make one of his signature shots, he would have stopped the boy immediately and retrained him to shoot according to the accepted style. Yet Doodle was a high scorer and won many games for his team using his peculiar shooting style.

From 12:30 until school let out at 3:00, they practiced every afternoon—dribbling, passing, faking, ball handling, shooting, and learning which foot to jump off and why. Coach Story hammered them about shooting. Each player had to be an excellent shooter, and by "excellent shooter" he meant score while being closely guarded. After he gave them an assignment, he would watch them for a while and then leave them to practice it while he went inside the gym to work with the varsity. But before he left he always reminded them, "Do not do anything in practice that you would not do in a game."

After school, if their mothers did not have something for them to do, Doodle and Howie would often play one-on-one on the dirt court in front of Wagoner's until suppertime. After supper they would rush through their chores and then get together to play again until dark. When a full moon provided light for them, they often played late into the night.

Late one afternoon, Howie was practicing his shooting in front of Wagoner's when a stranger, a black man, stopped to buy some gas. He was traveling through to Fulton, Tennessee. He stood watching Howie for a few seconds and then said, "You are really good at handling that ball. I mean you are *really* good, being so young." Hungry for praise—he never got any at home or at school—Howie was thrilled. Knowing, too, that the old men sitting on the porch in front of the store had heard what the stranger said to him made him even happier.

During his early pep talks, Coach Story told the boys what a person has to do to achieve success in sports and his secret method of doing it. "You have to work hard to be better than your opponent. You have to set your mind to accomplish that goal." He explained, "You can set your mind just the same as you can set a clock. Yes, you can. Practice doing that and see what happens." He said that each of them had been born with special athletic ability that they could waste or perfect. Perfecting it should be their goal. He urged them to think about how good it would feel to be successful. "Imagine your-selves as the state basketball champions in 1952."

By the time Howie and Doodle were ninth graders, Coach Story decided to use them on the varsity team. Howie was so small that no uniform at the school fit him. Mary Lee had to cut an old uniform down to his size, but even then, it was still too big. Wearing that droopy outfit, Howie played his first varsity game during the Purchase Pennyrile Tournament held in the old Carr Health Build-ing on the campus of Murray State College. Cuba was playing Nor-tonville and trailing. When somebody passed the ball to Howie, he was in such a panic that he turned and tried to pass it right back to the same player, who had already turned away from him. He threw the ball—hitting that player in the middle of his back. When Howie realized what he had done, he sank to the floor and covered his face in shame.

Doodle did not fare much better in his first game as a varsity player against Wingo. He made four fouls in the first minute and was so upset he ran to his coach, pleading to be taken out. Coach Story told him, "Go back in. It won't take you long to get that other one." In his first game, Jimmie Webb was so frightened when he got the ball that he dribbled down to the wrong end of the court and scored a basket for the other side.

Usually during games Coach Story sat still on the bench with both feet flat on the floor, legs spread apart, his arms folded across his chest or his hands resting on his thighs. He often leaned forward, but he rarely stood up, and he never yelled. He knew his boys could tell by the look on his face what he was thinking. "If you make a mistake during a game, don't look at me! Just keep on going," he told them time and time again. Before the warm-up, he always insisted that his players not look down the court at their opponents because "it makes it look as if you're dreading to play them."

As the ninth-grade Cubs grew stronger, Coach Story had them

play against other junior varsity teams. Their first out-of-town game was with the older, more experienced ninth graders at Beadleton. The Beadleton gym was upstairs and had six posts on the ball court, three on each side. The ceiling was so low that the top of the backboard touched it. The Cubs could not put an arc on their shots or get used to driving around the posts. They lost by 6 points. Coach Story was unhappy with their performance; he shamed them by saying, "Well, I guess I was wrong. I thought you boys were going to be ball players."

After the Beadleton game, he trained them to be more flexible and prepared for any environment. He drilled them even harder on the fundamentals, having them practice throwing a ball, catching a pass, shooting a ball, and timing a rebound. He had them dribble for hours through a maze of chairs. He taught them to guard a player by watching his beltline and feet to predict which way he would move. He warned them to watch their opponent's eyes, too, because he might signal with them. Also, he insisted that they talk to the players they were guarding: "Say anything that will distract him!" Doodle perfected this tactic to the point where he sometimes made his opponent break out in laughter. One time much later, just as a game with Wickliffe was beginning, Doodle told opponent Phil Rollins, "Oh, Phil, you're so wonderful. I got a picture of you on my bedroom wall." The surprised Rollins ran down the court laughing.

One morning after their math class, Jack Story stood silently in front of the window staring out of a smudged windowpane. He was looking at the gravel road that ran alongside the school and led to Highway 303. Wondering what he was looking at, Joe Buddy, Jimmie, Raymon, Howie, and Doodle, dressed in their usual attire—clean but double-patched overalls, faded shirts, and worn, hand-me-down shoes—gathered on either side of him. After what seemed to them a long silence, the coach told them to look down the road and said, "You can't see very far down it, but you can go pretty

far down it. You can go to Pilot Oak or to Mayfield—or you can go
to Louisville, Cincinnati, Detroit, or to New York City. Those places
sound pretty far away to you now. Well, I don't aim for us to go that
far away. I am aiming for us to go to Lexington, Kentucky, to play
in the state basketball tournament. That's where I'm aiming for us to
go in '52." He looked at their young, innocent faces and concluded
quietly, "But whether or not we go is up to you. It's up to you."

Young as they were, they did not fully understand everything
he told them, but they understood him well enough to know that he
liked the same things they did. And what Coach Story wanted was
fun to them. Getting out of class and study hall every afternoon to
practice basketball was more fun than they had ever imagined they
would have at school. Practicing was not work to them. They loved it.

Until Jack Story came into their lives, they had had no one to
talk to them about how important it is to dream or to set goals and
work step by step to achieve them. And the idea of being "honored"
for doing what they loved—playing basketball—was hard to believe.
All their parents had ever done was to complain about their playing
basketball. All their parents ever talked about was getting the crops
in and out, feeding the livestock, milking the cows, cleaning the
fencerow and the barn, topping tobacco and praying that enough
would be made from the tobacco sale to get them through the winter. Their parents, for the most part, were not the kind of people
who talked about achieving success and certainly not by playing basketball. Some of them were like Howie's parents, who did not even
know that athletic scholarships to colleges were available to their
youngsters. For them, just getting through the day was challenging
enough. Although they were hard workers, some much more so than
others, few of them had any far-reaching ambition.

Coach Story knew early on that Howie and Doodle had the
most star potential among the players. He also knew that they were
sons of sharecroppers who did not always make ends meet, no mat-

ter how hard they worked. Although the parents of the other boys were not well off, they all had jobs in addition to their farming, jobs that provided a small but steady income. Sharecroppers never had a steady income. They had nothing to count on—not the weather, not the crops, not the landlord who could and often did make life even harder for them.

Sharecroppers were the poorest of the poor, and yet their young children were not aware of their poverty until they got to be teenagers. Sensitive to their living conditions, Jack Story paid Howie and Doodle for doing jobs around the school, such as painting the cafeteria and the hallway. In the summers during their last two years in high school, he got them jobs at the Pet Milk company in Mayfield and he allowed them to board in his home.

Coach Story wanted to keep them in school playing basketball so they would get athletic scholarships to colleges. College would open the doors to the outside world for them. He insisted they keep up with their school assignments even though the demands he made on their time might have suggested otherwise. Their high school education was essential not only to getting into college but also to succeeding once they were there. No college coach wants an athlete who is unable to make his grades and therefore unable to maintain his eligibility.

18

Skull Sessions

The beginning is the most important part of the work.
—Plato

Coach Story expected his team to behave in a proper manner at all times. Although he well understood that boys will be boys, he let them know that they were *to act right.* He talked to them about what it means to be an athlete, stressing that an athlete plays fair. He never cheats. He wins by outplaying his opponent. And he never underestimates his opponent's strength. Story warned them often about going into a game thinking that they were in for an easy time. On more than one occasion, he had seen signs of arrogance in them, so he emphasized how dangerous it is to underestimate an opponent.

He told them they were never ever to talk back to a referee. If you lose, lose like a man, he would say. Don't complain or whine. Don't make excuses. And do not blame the officials, or the other guys. He advised them not to grieve over their mistakes but to learn from them, figure out what they had done wrong so they would not do the same thing again. Whenever they won, he wanted them to win graciously—"Do not brag!" He said that there is nothing worse than a bigheaded winner or a sore loser. They were to be polite and grateful. Either way—win or lose—he wanted to see them shake hands with their opponents and pat them on the back. If they lost, it meant the other team had outplayed them, and he wanted them to tell the winners that. "You congratulate them," he said. And whenever someone said something hateful to them, they were to be silent. Coach instructed them to walk on by without looking at people who insulted them.

He harped on how important it was that they improve themselves in every way—not just in athletics. He wanted them to study and learn, to keep their word if they promised someone something, to tell the truth, and to show respect for others. He wanted them to be not only winners but also men of good character. He gave countless examples of individuals and teams that had overcome great odds and succeeded. Think of them as your role models, he would say.

He also taught them how important it was to take good care of themselves physically. He made them feel grownup when he handed each boy a jock strap and explained the value of wearing one. He insisted that they dry their necks and backs well after sweating or showering to avoid catching colds, and he warned them against washing their hair with hot water, saying that would make their hair fall out! He told them to keep themselves clean, brush their teeth twice a day, get plenty of rest, and not to smoke.

He was vehemently opposed to smoking, believing it was unhealthy long before others did, and forbade it, although smoking was not only very popular but actually fashionable in the 1940s and '50s, and particularly so in this region that raised tobacco. On trips to out-of-town games, he usually made the boys he suspected of smoking ride with him.

The folks in the community kept their eyes on the basketball players in more than one way. One day, old "Bear" Wiggins, a well-known "bird dog" (someone who tattles) told Coach Story that he had seen Joe Buddy smoking a cigarette in back of Wagoner's store. Although Coach Story never laid down rules about what the boys were to eat or drink, or when to go to bed, he would not allow smoking. Oddly enough though, he never complained if they chewed tobacco. He must have thought doing so was the lesser of two evils. He even provided spit cans, which he stationed around the gym floor. Except for Howie, the others occasionally smoked cigarettes, but they all regularly chewed an inexpensive brand called Days Work, a tobacco that the local farmers twisted themselves.

The day Jack Story confronted him about smoking, Joe Buddy said, the coach stared at him through narrow slits of eyes and told him, "You cannot smoke and play basketball for me. Smoking cuts your wind off. It keeps you from running. I cannot use you! I am suspending you for three weeks from practice. Meanwhile, you can think about which one you want to do—smoke or play basketball." He turned quickly and walked away. Joe Buddy was dumbstruck. He had thought he was too important to the team to be suspended and wondered how the coach was going to get along without him. Much to his dismay, he soon learned that coach got along just fine. After that suspension, Joe's fondness for cigarettes disappeared.

When Joe Buddy's pal Ted got into trouble, Ted said that Coach Story taught him a lesson, too. In a game with Kirksey, during the third quarter, for some inexplicable reason, Ted was standing under the basket by himself—"snowbirding," as it was called. Except for one opposing player who was a foot taller than Ted, no one else was near him. One of the Cubs threw the ball the length of the court to Ted, who caught it, looked over his shoulder, and saw his opponent standing there. With his back to the goal, Ted threw the ball backward—over his head—and missed the basket. Coach Story pulled him out of the game immediately.

The next day at practice, he sent the team outside to run but instructed Ted to stay to the side of the goal and tossed him a basketball, saying curtly, "Shoot the ball." Ted shot it and missed. The coach told him to shoot it again and to keep shooting it until he came back. He left the gym. Almost an hour later, he returned and asked Ted if he had missed any baskets. Ted replied yes. Nodding his head affirmatively, Coach Story told him again to keep on shooting until he came back. Ted got so tired he could hardly lift the ball, but he was afraid to rest for fear that Coach Story was watching him from someplace in the gym. Finally, when the school bell rang and it was time for the children to board the buses for home, Coach Story reappeared and asked again if Ted had missed any more baskets. He sorrowfully answered, "Yes, sir, I have." Coach Story explained, "The lesson I am teaching you is this: when you get to the point where you cannot miss a shot when you are looking at the basket, then you can shoot over your head without looking at it."

After watching Raymon let a player dribble around him one day, Coach Story reprimanded him, saying that if Raymon let a guy dribble around him again, he could head for the bench and stay there. During practices and even during games, lovesick Jimmie Webb would oftentimes be looking around for Martha Lou Casey instead of paying attention to instructions. Although Coach Story would get annoyed with Jimmie, he usually did not say too much to him, probably because Jimmie had an endearing, innocent quality that made criticizing him difficult.

However, at one of the games, Coach Story finally lost his patience, and he taught Jimmie an unforgettable lesson. Coach told him, "I want you to get under the basket and then come back out and get in the corner. We'll try to get the ball to you so you can shoot a jump shot from there. Do you understand what you're to do?" Still watching the bleachers, Jimmie mumbled, "Yes, sir," but Coach Story knew the boy had been daydreaming the whole time

Jack and Mary Lee Story in front of Cuba School. (Photo courtesy of Barbara Story Crowell.)

he was talking to him. Shocking everyone present, he closed his fist and banged it hard up and down under Jimmie's chin two or three times, making the boy's teeth slam together and his head hurt. From then on, Jimmie remained alert.

Other tips Coach Story taught the boys included learning how to dribble the basketball with their fingertips rather than with the palms of their hands, so it would not slip. He also taught them a way to bend their thumbs back to strengthen their wrists and urged them to practice this finger exercise while sitting in class listening to their teachers.

After the first few times of watching them walk and run, he told them that if they wanted to be ball players, they needed to stop walking like one-legged ducks. The boys remembered the coach saying, "Learn to walk right, so you'll run right. Do not run slew-footed! You lose some of your power if you don't push off with your toes." During their first practice session on that dirt road behind the school, all they did for nearly two hours was to walk with their toes pointed straight ahead.

Coach reminded them that their objective was to throw the ball through the hoop and their opponent's objective was to prevent them from doing that. He would go on to explain, "In order to get a decent shot, you have to fool him. You've to make him think you are going one way when you are really going another way. You have to learn lots of ways to fake him. You can fake with your hands, head, waist, legs, and eyes." Then he would throw the ball without looking in the direction he was throwing it and hit one of them, purposely startling the unsuspecting target to make his point. Next he would call one of the boys onto the court to demonstrate some faking techniques. After his demonstration, he would leave them to practice faking for an hour. Doodle and Howie were especially good with this faking technique.

The boys listened intently to whatever he told them, but Howie, ambitious to learn all he could, took every word to heart. If Coach Story told the team to practice a certain exercise for a certain number of times, Howie practiced three times longer. He practiced until he had it perfected. While they were outside in the schoolyard one day, Coach Story told Howie to run as fast as he could from where they were standing at the back of school to the road. Coach Story tossed a basketball to him and told him, "Now run back to me with the ball as fast as you can." Howie could not run with the ball as fast as he could without it. Coach Story told him, "Practice until you are able to run fast either way." Before long, Howie could.

Coach Story devised many simple ways for teaching his players how to pass, shoot, dribble, and rebound. One of his shooting drills was to have them put one hand in a back pocket and shoot with the other. Then he would have them switch hands. He made them dribble through an obstacle course of wooden chairs. He would set a chair at the free-throw line and make the boys dribble up to it. They had to run straight toward the chair for a jump shot without banging into the chair.

One afternoon while they were scrimmaging in practice, Jimmie Webb threw a pass that accidentally hit Coach Story in the head as he sat on the bleachers. "I thought for sure I'd be killed or sent home," Jimmie said, "but he said nothing to me, just went on like nothing had happened. Unintentional mistakes like that were the *only* ones he ignored, though."

Using the road behind the school, Coach Story trained the boys to develop their peripheral vision. He taught them to walk holding their heads and backs straight, pointing their toes straight ahead, while they stooped to pick up handfuls of rocks to throw from behind their backs at trees. He wanted them to learn to see without looking, to hit those trees without turning their heads in the direction they were aiming.

Howie loved the visual exercise and practiced it just about everywhere he went. People in Pilot Oak were amused when they first noticed the fifteen-year-old, no taller or wider than a bed slat (that is how they described him), walk ramrod straight along the road, hitting one tree after another without looking. The old folks thought he was a sight to watch. Born with superb eye-hand coordination, Howie mastered this skill easily. While in the classroom, he practiced seeing without looking who was sitting on either side of him, and he knew what each person was doing. He developed exceptional peripheral vision, an ability that gave him a great advantage coming down the court on a fast break. He could run down the court and know where all the players were and what they were doing without looking at them. Such court sense is rare among basketball players.

Coach Story arranged for them to play other eighth-grade

teams in the area, and they did well. Then he held intramural tournaments, pitting eighth graders against ninth and even tenth graders. When they beat those older players, he grinned, knowing that
his championship team was blooming. Although they hungered for
praise, he never gave it. He was never demonstrative, but they got to
the point where they could read his face. They knew by the way he
watched them play if they were doing well, and pleasing him made
them feel good.

As ninth graders, the team had to practice every afternoon
from 12:30 to 3:00, and then ride the bus home. After the bus let
Howie and Doodle out at the store in Pilot Oak, they would often
get the basketball from Mr. Wagoner and play in front of the store
until suppertime, joining the older boys, who looked forward to
playing with them. Doodle had a nearly three-mile walk home, so
he did not play as late as Howie, who lived just across the street from
the dirt court. Unless his mother allowed him to spend the night
with the Crittendens, Doodle would have to run home in order to
arrive before his dad came in from the fields. A few times when
Doodle did not get home early enough, his father was angry. Vodie
believed that his son's playing ball was a sign of shiftlessness and
irresponsibility. He never saw it as a means to perfect a skill that
would later lead his son to a better life. Doodle withstood his father's
lectures and his whippings and kept on playing.

He and Howie played in all kinds of weather. In the winter they would be out in front of the store playing with their hats,
coats, gloves, and boots on. It was sometimes so cold their hands
would hurt handling the basketball as they bounced it off the frozen ground. When the ground thawed and got muddy, they had to
wear working boots in order to play. They would slip, slide, and fall
in the mud, laughing. They did their best not to get the basketball
too dirty but cared less about their clothes and hands.

Even though the old gymnasium in the Pilot Oak School was

not in good shape, the principal, Mr. Douglas, refused to let the boys practice in it when school was not in session. Determined to get into the school secretly, they discovered a way. By standing on Doodle's shoulders, Howie could reach a windowsill, remove the loose pane in the window, and crawl through the opening. Once he was inside the building, he unlocked the back door for Doodle. Within seconds they would have a good basketball and the whole place to themselves.

In the summertime, with his windows open, Mr. Douglas, who lived next door to the school, would hear the ball bouncing in the gym and run the boys off. But his threats never deterred them. They never stole or damaged anything; they just played basketball in the gym. The only time they ever got scared was the time the candy closet at school was robbed. Though not guilty, they worried that they would be accused. They were not accused and even that scare did not prevent them from playing in the gym.

Howie and Doodle were unique among the boys on the team because they competed with each other. They motivated and challenged each other about everything. When it was just the two of them playing ball, they would argue about playing full-court or half-court. Howie liked to play a full-court basketball game because he was fast and could beat Doodle every time. Doodle liked to play a half-court game where he had the advantage of his height. They argued which way they were going to play first, and then they would play a game each way.

19

Unforgettable Cayce

Everything is funny as long as it is happening to someone else.
—Will Rogers

In the summer of 1949 the state highway department blacktopped the gravel road, Highway 303, running from Mayfield to Cuba to Pilot Oak. Howie and Doodle were ecstatic. They finally had a hard surface on which to play ball when they could not play in the gym. In the stillness of hazy summer afternoons, many of the folks in Pilot Oak could hear that basketball pounding on the pavement. As usual, when the moon was full, the boys played late into the night—and in all kinds of weather. This year-round outdoor competition, even in the deepest winter, primed them for playing in all conditions.

By the time school started, Doodle was larger than the others in his sophomore class and thought he knew much more than he actually did. He started skipping morning classes to hitchhike to Mayfield to play pool with some older boys. But no matter what his mornings were like, he was always at school in time for lunch, and he stayed for basketball practice.

Sometimes he could slip into the gym through the back entrance without Coach Story realizing that he had been absent all morning. The gym was in the center of the school building and had classrooms on both sides; study hall and the library were at one end and Coach Story's office at the other end, in the front of the building.

After Mrs. Warner, an English teacher and a strict one, too, informed Coach Story that Doodle was often absent from her class without an excuse and that he and a couple of others on the team were failing her course, a grim-faced Coach Story told those boys that they had to pass *all* of their classes in order to stay on the team. More than anything else in the world, Doodle wanted to play basketball. The hardwood was his stage. Playing ball made him feel happy and important; he could not live, he said, without being on the team. Although he knew that Coach Story needed him to play, he also knew that he would suspend him. At that point, one of his friends in class, Donald Poyner, came to his rescue.

Coach Story relied on Donald for many small jobs because the boy was smart and had good judgment. A small, thin boy with dark hair and dark brown eyes, Donald was nicknamed Central Intelligence. He was thought by some to be intellectually and academically far ahead of his classmates and even of some teachers. When one of the older teachers could not keep his record book for homeroom and classroom organized, Coach Story had Donald help him straighten the records out and keep them for the teacher the rest of the year. When the agriculture teacher in charge of the Future Farmers of America (FFA) chapter had shown no interest in developing the organization, Coach Story told Donald to skip agriculture classes and spend his time improving the chapter. Under the boy's leadership, Cuba's FFA chapter was awarded the State Gold Emblem for excellence.

Cuba's senior class officers in 1951–1952. Each had close ties to the basketball team. Pictured left to right are class reporter Howie Crittenden, treasurer Martha (Casey) Webb, president Donald Poyner, secretary Carolyn Work, and vice president Joe Buddy Warren. (Cuba School yearbook photo.)

Donald's intelligence was acknowledged throughout the Cuba–Pilot Oak area. One story concerning him and one of the old store setters involved a new set of *World Book* encyclopedias the boy received for Christmas in 1947. Often a visitor in the Poyners' home, the old man noticed Donald's habit of reading. Pauline Harper, the store owner, said that one day one of the old store setters at her place announced, "That Donald ought to be smart because he's got his head stuck in dem sack-a-peters all the time."

The Pilot Oak general store where people in the community shopped and congregated to socialize, gossip, and listen to Cubs basketball games on the radio. Nearby was a dirt basketball court where the Cubs often played and honed their skills. (Photo courtesy of Charles Floyd.)

When Donald asked Coach Story if it would help if he arranged to get a few classmates to volunteer to tutor those players who needed help keeping up with the classroom work they had missed while playing ball, Coach Story answered with a resounding yes. The boys were more than happy to work with their female peers. Several courtships began when tutees fell in love with their tutors. Martha Lou Casey, a lovely straight-A student with a perfect attendance record, was in love with Jimmie Webb, who adored her. Martha saw to it that his work and hers were done to perfection. Raymon had a crush on the girl assigned to help him. Joe Buddy and Ted were delighted to learn who their tutors were. However, Doodle, smitten by pretty Julia Harris, wanted her to assist him, and he was very upset when Coach Story told him to forget that idea because he had already appointed Donald to tutor him.

Cubs cheerleaders (left to right) Barbara Harper, Carolyn Work, and Martha (Casey) Webb rest their vocal cords outside Harper's Grocery. (Photo courtesy of Donald Poyner.)

During the early part of the 1949–1950 basketball season, the Cubs garnered an impressive string of victories playing against the other schools in Graves County. By now the word had spread that the boys had perfected not only their fundamental skills but also their Harlem Globetrotters routine. They were a sight to see! People from all over the county and adjacent counties came to watch them play. At that time the second, or the B, team played after the varsity played. But when word got out that Coach Story's B team was better than his varsity, people came to root for the B team and skipped out on the varsity games. Although the players were making a name for themselves as a team to watch, they were not yet ready to play big schools such as Paducah Tilghman and Owensboro Senior High.

Once the Cubs announced their intention to win the state

championship in 1952, people in Cuba and in Pilot Oak began thinking, Well, yes, maybe. The entire student body adopted the team's mission statement and spread it throughout the community. Although not accustomed to hearing their youngsters say that they had a goal they were working toward achieving, the people stopped speaking of *if* the boys won and began saying what a grand day it would be *when* their boys won the state championship!

The Cubs loved being the topic of conversation at the local stores and in the churchyards and as far away as Paducah, Mayfield, and Murray. Someone would ask if everyone had noticed how much Doodle had grown over the summer and say that he should tear them up this year. And how about Howie! He was running faster than a rabbit. Why, nobody would be able to take the ball away from that boy anymore, they said.

By late summer 1949, Doodle and Howie wanted nothing to do with farm work and had decided that if they worked harder at their basketball they could go to the state tournament the next year instead of waiting for their senior year. When Willie ordered Howie out to top their two-acre patch of tobacco, Doodle went along to help. Topping tobacco is a tedious, dirty, time-consuming task that requires cutting the top off every single tobacco plant except the few that are left to collect seeds from later. Topping tobacco prevents the plant from flowering and helps it leaf out broadly. The boys despised the work, and to ease their job they took a basketball to the field with them. They decided to get the job finished as quickly as possible. Instead of topping the tobacco in a neat, uniform manner, as it should be done, they ran down the rows, each boy topping two rows at a time. At the end of the rows, they would practice ball handling, then they would turn and go back, topping two more rows each. When they were done, the field had an uneven, messy, zigzaggy look, with some rows of plants much taller than others and many plants left untopped. It looked, as the store setters exclaimed, as if a drunkard had topped it. Old Willie Crittenden was burned up about it and the teasing he had to endure.

During their one-on-one sessions, Howie and Doodle developed skills on their own. Without any instruction from Coach Story, they perfected different plays by practicing in the fields, on the roads, and in front of Wagoner's. By the time they were in the tenth grade, they had played together for so long that each knew precisely where the other would be on the court in a game. For one thing, Doodle, the center, and Howie, a guard, learned to make perfect blind passes. Howie would throw the ball to Doodle and then cut right across in front of him and run to the basket. Doodle would fake as if he were going to shoot a hook shot or pass the ball to somebody else. All the while Doodle knew exactly where Howie was going and would make a blind pass to him.

In actual games, on a rebound shot, Doodle would tip the ball out to the side. Howie would know which way Doodle would tip the ball from where he was on the court and would position himself to catch it. Then the two of them would be off and gone on a fast break. When their opponents shot a free throw and missed, the Cubs would tap the ball to the side, and Joe Buddy or Howie would go get the ball, turn, look for a man running down the court, and hit him in the middle of the court. Then they would be on a fast break again.

For Christmas 1949, W. A. mailed his younger brother a basketball, the finest one he could buy. It was the first real basketball Howie had ever owned and he was thrilled to have it. On Christmas morning, sleet was coming down in sheets. Four inches of snow already covered the ground. It was impossible to work or play outside. Howie hugged the new ball, spun it around on his finger, and threw it up in the air several times. Then he began quietly throwing it over the opened door between the kitchen and living room and catching it when it bounced off the floor. Willie, in his rocking chair in the living room, watched silently for a while. Suddenly he jumped out of his chair, angrily snatched the ball from the boy's hand, and limped into the kitchen as Howie protested. Then Willie flung the back door open and threw the ball as far as he could out into the yard, ordering Howie to sit down and be quiet. Howie's eyes filled with tears. Fearing the ball might be ruined, he begged his father to let him go get it. Willie returned to his rocking chair, refusing to look at his son and mumbling he was going to teach that boy a lesson. Tearfully, Howie looked at his mother, who stood leaning against the kitchen window, staring at the ball as it gradually disappeared behind the film of sleet. Willie closed his eyes as if to nap. Silently, Alta Ruth wrapped her woolen shawl around her head and shoulders, slipped out the back door, ran into the yard, picked the ball up, and handed it to Howie, who stood in the doorway with Helen, watching. No word passed between mother and son as they pressed the basketball between them for a moment. From then on, Howie hid the ball under his bed.

At the start of their sophomore year, the Cubs were good and they knew it. They had many adoring fans and pretty girls swarming around them. Basketball had become the most important thing in their lives, exactly what Coach Story had wanted to happen.

When they advanced to the 1949–1950 regional tournaments at Murray State, they played the opening round in Cayce, Kentucky, home of Casey Jones, the famed locomotive engineer who lost his life in a train wreck. Two weeks earlier in the district tournaments, the Cubs had thoroughly whipped Cayce, 92-36, in Cayce's gym. Doodle had scored 52 points. When the regional game came up, the Cubs were overly confident, despite Coach Story's admonitions. They had just received new uniforms and for the first time had warm-ups suits. Although they were only sophomores, they had no doubts about their going to the state tournament that year, and they were enthusiastic and eager to go. But a day or so before March 9, when the game was to be played, Coach Story learned that two of Cuba's starters, Don Stone, a senior, and Raymon, who was a sophomore, were unable to play in this opening round. Raymon had the mumps, and Don had an injured knee. Although Coach Story was concerned about losing these two players, the other Cubs were not. In fact, Doodle boasted that he, Howie, Joe Buddy, Jimmie Webb, and Ted, with one hand tied behind them, could lick little Cayce easily.

As the high scorer on his team, Doodle felt immensely superior to the Cayce boys. Seeing Coach Story standing at the other end of the gym with his back turned talking with some men, Doodle decided to entertain the crowd for a few minutes before the game started. He strutted in front of the bleachers, boasting loudly about how Cuba was going to whip poor little Cayce that night. The crowd's laughter egged him on, and he proceeded to berate his opponents, saying, "I hate to play a little outfit like Cayce! They're pitiful." He even asked Cayce players if they were scared, telling them that they looked scared and that they ought to be scared, too, if they remembered what Cuba had done to them the last time the two teams played. Some of the Cayce players chuckled, while others looked at Doodle with disgust. But the audience laughed.

At one point Doodle lifted his long hairy leg, flaunting his new shoes, and, pointing to his new gold and green warm-up suit, asking the Cayce boys if they were jealous. Sensing that everyone, except the Cayce fans, of course, was in a jovial mood, Doodle ended his performance by telling his opponents, "You all look like a scared cat in a room full of rocking chairs." Doodle was so engaged with his comic act he never glanced at the coach. If he had, he would have melted like the wicked witch. Coach Story was sitting silently with his arms folded and his chin on his chest, grinding his teeth ever so slightly as he listened to his top scorer.

Doodle entered the Cayce game as if it were some kind of joke. During the entire first half, he goofed off, letting Cayce score, thinking that he and his buddies could turn up the heat and burn Cayce out anytime they got ready. Every so often in the first half, Doodle would put his hand to his ear, cock his head to the side, and call out to the crowd, "Who's ahead?" The audience would shout back "Cayce!" and laugh. The Cuba partisans found his act amusing, believing also that the Cubs could run the score up in their favor whenever they got ready.

At the end of the first half, as he was going to the locker room, Doodle asked again who was ahead and the crowd laughingly yelled, "Cayce! Cayce!—42-37!" Nearly everyone that night was having a great time.

The second half started. Coach Story said nothing. Cayce scored again, but the Cubs were still having too much fun to go into action and were going to hold off scoring a little while longer to make their final lunge more dramatic and exciting. Coach Story knew what was going to happen, and he let it happen. When the Cubs got ready to score, they could not. Before they realized it, the clock ran out and the final answer to "Who's ahead?" was "Cayce!" Doodle could not believe it. Cayce, of all teams, had given Cuba a shellacking that Cuba would never forget. Stunned, embarrassed, and full of self-doubt, Doodle and his cohorts left the floor dejectedly. None of them dared to look at Coach Story.

The next day, the whole county was laughing about the game. Doodle felt wretched and so did the others. Cuba had lost to Cayce, of all teams, and lost because of their own foolishness. Doodle had scored only 4 points that night; he was so embarrassed. They all were embarrassed. Jack Story never said a single word to Doodle or any of the others about that game. The result spoke for itself. He figured it would do those boys good to learn a few things the painful way. What may have been the saddest thing of all was that they had blown their chance to go to the state tournament as sophomores.

In all their years of playing together, they never had a lower moment or a more humbling experience than that Cayce game. It haunted them for a long time.

20

Different Encounters

Youth is the season made for joy.
—John Gay

The Cubs entered their junior year slightly more subdued and matured, with the weight of great expectations upon them. They were not promising underclassmen anymore. They were the varsity now—the Cuba Cubs. When the school year started in the fall of 1950, the changes in all of them were noticeable. They had grown taller and more muscular. Only one had a problem—Raymon was having serious ankle pain. Without his defense and rebounding, the team could not be as successful as it had been. Worriedly, Coach Story started looking around for a backup. He found one in Bill Pollock, who played basketball for Fancy Farm, about ten miles from Mayfield.

A six-foot-two, dark-haired, handsome boy, Bill lived in Dublin, near the Catholic community of Fancy Farm, where he attended school. Although Coach Story did not usually recruit players, he negotiated through Bill's mother's cousin, who lived in Cuba. When this relative approached Bill about transferring to the Cuba School to play basketball, Bill did not object. As the only Protestant boy in a school where all the classes were taught by nuns, he was more than willing to switch. Although he continued to live at home in Dublin, he transferred as a junior to Cuba. According to the rules, he was not allowed to play ball for a year after transferring, but as a manager, he traveled with the Cubs and practiced with them daily. He did not play in any games in the 1950–1951 season, but as a senior, Bill turned out to be a valuable sixth man who filled in admirably for Raymon and for Doodle.

The Cubs' prowess on the hardwood was the leading topic of conversation, not just at Harper's, Rhodes', and Wagoner's, but at all the other stores in Graves County. Discussions about crops, politics, illnesses, and deaths were quickly replaced with talk about what Jack Story and his team were going to do next. The Cubs games were so popular that crowds packed the gyms. Some home games were moved to other schools that had larger gyms, like Mayfield's and Sedalia's, but the majority of games were played at the Cuba School.

As the team became more and more famous, a large number of fans had to be turned away for lack of space in the Cuba gym, so a balcony was built above the bleachers, adding three more rows of seats. Folding chairs were placed on the stage at the end of the gym's playing floor. With these additional seating arrangements, the gym could seat 450, but as many as 500 to 550 crowded in. Still, many others had to be turned away. The court was ten or so feet short of official length anyway (yes, that's true), and with fans standing practically on the playing floor, the Cubs got used to playing in crowded and smoky conditions. (No laws in the 1950s prohibited smoking.)

The games started at 7:00 p.m., and people would start lining up outside the school by 5:00. Coach Story usually arrived around 6:00 to open the doors. About that same time Em Boyd Poyner, Donald's dad and Cuba's official ticket agent, would come directly from his work at the Mayfield Merit Clothing Company, without even stopping to eat supper.

Jess, Joe Buddy's dad, never missed a game or a practice. In fact, the joke was that Jess had a better attendance record at school than his son. None of the fathers of the other Cubs attended any of the games at this time. With all the hoopla that surrounded the players, especially Doodle, Howie, and Jimmie Webb, it would be logical to assume that their parents would have been so proud of their sons that they would be first in line for admission. But that was not the case.

One evening when the Cubs were playing Lowes, Doodle was surprised at halftime when someone shouted to him that his dad was there. Vodie and two men were riding home from Mayfield, where they had part-time jobs and, Vodie said, the other guys wanted to stop to see how the ball game was turning out. They stayed only a few minutes, but it was long enough for Vodie to hear his son praised and to wave hello to him.

With girls swooning and swooping around the ball players, the boys' temptation to swagger was strong. And, at times, their success with basketball and with girls made them forgetful of their coach's cautionary advice. In Mayfield late one night, a policeman went to the Storys' home, apologized for waking Coach Story up, and said he thought the coach ought to know what his boys had been doing. He explained he had just stopped some of the Cubs riding recklessly around town in an old topless heap that had no license, no windshield, no lights, and no brakes. And the only way the doors opened was from the outside. Having seen that heap before, Coach Story groaned and hung his head as he listened.

The policeman explained that driving without brakes was not the only dangerous problem. The shift had three forward gears and a reverse, but it would not stay in gear unless the driver held it in the gear he wanted. Otherwise it popped back into neutral. So Jimmie Webb, the owner of the vehicle, was driving holding the gear stick in one hand and the steering wheel in the other while two other boys held flashlights so Jimmie could see the road.

When the policeman first saw the boys they were in downtown Mayfield on the north side of the courthouse. As they traveled

Howie and Joe Buddy enjoy the beach at Kentucky Lake the summer of 1951 before returning to school for one more year of basketball. (Photo courtesy of Joe Buddy Warren.)

uphill on the courthouse square, singing at the top of their lungs, the motor died. The car started coasting backward fast, in a weaving, unstable fashion. Unable to stop it or even slow it down, they rolled backward all the way down the hill and through a red light, barely missing another automobile. They were all scared to death when they heard the siren and saw the police car bearing down on them. The policeman assured Coach Story that the boys had not been drinking, just having a big time. He did not give them a ticket but believed he had "scared the hell out of them." He warned them that neither he nor any of the other policemen in Mayfield had better ever see them driving recklessly or in that pile of junk again.

21

Pride before Another Fall

Of all the animals, the boy is the most unmanageable.
—Plato

The Cubs opened the 1950–1951 season with two big wins: one over
Lowes, 81-48, and the other over Cayce (again), 75-36. As juniors
with an enviable reputation, they were preening like rock stars the
night they were scheduled to play at Lynn Grove, a nearby small,
poorly built rural school. Although they had not forgotten the Cayce
game the year before, their memory of it had dimmed some. On the
day they were to play Lynn Grove, they did not see any harm in having a little fun.

For days before the game, the southern end of the county had
been hit with a torrential downpour. The day of the game, rain still
poured steadily in opaque sheets. The gym at Lynn Grove had been
built on ground level without a foundation. In hard rains, the water
seeped through the gym floor and washed across it. Knowing the
conditions of this gym, and believing they were far superior to their

competition, Howie, Doodle, Joe Buddy, Ted, and Jimmie Webb decided to dress for the occasion.

They never had practice on game days, just skull sessions during which Coach Story would talk to them about plays. As soon as he dismissed them that afternoon, they changed clothes. They put on bib overalls, straw hats, and green rubber hip boots (the ones they wore duck hunting). With black shoe polish, they painted "Cuba" all over their hip boots. Outfitted to mock their opponents, they piled into an old 1936 Model A Ford that Doodle had borrowed from his brother Bill.

The car had a '38 transmission, a '42 motor, and mechanical brakes that had been changed to hydraulic ones. The original seats had been replaced with seats from an old couch. The front of the car was all exposed; it did not have a hood. The muffler had gone out, and so Bill had taken a weld pipe and bent it to meet the curvature of the axle. That way, anyone riding inside the car could not hear the awful noise it was making, but people for miles around sure could.

As they were driving along the country road making a tremendous racket, they were confident and happy, singing,

> Irene, goodnight, Irene, goodnight,
> Goodnight, Irene, goodnight, Irene,
> I'll see you in my dreams.
> Sometimes I live in the country,
> Sometimes I live in town,
> Sometimes I have a great notion to jump into the river
>   and drown.
> Irene, goodnight, Irene. I'll see you in my dreams.

Without a doubt in their minds that they could conquer the world, they were simply unable to resist an opportunity to show off their power. They stopped at the store in Lynn Grove to buy soft drinks,

No player captured the crowd's fancy the way Doodle did. Irrepressible and irresistible, he loved to make people laugh, and his brown eyes sparkled with mischief. (Photo courtesy of Charles Floyd.)

and Doodle immediately made himself the center of attention. Chewing on an unlit cigar, he strutted around, greeting the customers and the store setters. To one of the old guys dressed in obviously new denim overalls and a red plaid shirt, Doodle said that he looked like a third-Monday mule. They all laughed.

That remark was a genial expression, a compliment of sorts, said among the old-timers to a person who was dressed nicely. The expression stemmed from the time when farmers went to Trade Day in Mayfield on the third Monday in March. Some farmers claimed that a few dishonest traders were skilled at doing cosmetic work on their mules' teeth before they attempted to trade them. Usually, a good mule trader can estimate an animal's age by examining his teeth, but not always. As one of the farmers said, it is as difficult to tell a mule's age sometimes as it is to tell a pretty woman's. He went on to explain that a few of these traders could make an old mule's teeth appear somewhat like those of a younger animal, and they earned good money doing it. An old mule that had been allowed to rest a few days and had had his teeth cleaned would look pretty good. Hence the expression—You look like a third-Monday mule.

The mood in the store darkened once Doodle asked if anyone around there played basketball. Such a question was rude. Why, everyone knew that Lynn Grove had a team. A lively discussion ensued for nearly half an hour, making the boys late getting to their destination. Their intentions to change their clothes before Coach Story saw them were dashed. When they arrived at the school, he was standing by the coal stove in one corner of the gym looking angry; he did not tolerate tardiness. When he saw his boys dressed in those outfits, the scowl on his face told them they were in trouble. He ordered them to hurry up and get dressed.

The Lynn Grove team was not good at all. The Cubs should have beaten them by 40 points at least, but the final score was 63-40. Worrying about how angry Coach was with them, the starters could not concentrate and play well. By the end of the third quarter, Coach Story was so fed up with the way they were playing that he ordered Howie, Doodle, Joe Buddy, and Jimmie Webb out of the game and told them to get dressed. Red-faced, they sat on the bench, scrunched down with shame, as they watched Raymon, Bill, Paul, Jimmy Jones, and Jimmy Brown finish and win in the last quarter.

After Lynn Grove, the Cubs defeated Melber 93-42, Fancy Farm 59-40, and Sedalia 71-44, making six consecutive wins. The next game was one in which the Farmington team opened with a slowdown, a ball-control technique. Cuba got the lead and responded by holding the ball and putting on a Globetrotter show, winning the game 22–10. Then came wins over Murray, 60-27, Symsonia, 58-35, and Fulton, 66–50, giving Cuba a perfect 10-0 start.

During the Graves County Christmas Tournament, the Cubs defeated Symsonia 47-3, Wingo 74-50, and Sedalia 66-39. From there they went to the Paducah Christmas Tournament, a prestigious competition. In the opening round, the Cubs defeated Hardin 52-40 for their fourteenth consecutive win of the season. Then in the second tournament game—their sixth game in a week—the Cubs played what was to be their worst game of the entire season. They were very tired before the game even started due to an unacceptable reason.

The night before they were to play Cave-in-Rock, the five starters, without Coach Story's knowledge, much less his permission, walked several miles from their motel to another section of Paducah. They were searching for 808 Washington Street where, they had been told, were some older girls with whom they could have a lot of fun. They knew nothing about such places, much less about older girls, so they were curious and naive. They knew nothing about Paducah either and may have walked ten or more miles out of their way searching for the place. After they finally found their destination, they debated whether or not to go inside. At last, they nervously entered the reception room and were shocked when told the fee for admission. Excusing themselves politely, they stepped back outside, whispering anxiously as they stood on the sidewalk, discussing what to do. Briefly they considered returning to the motel, but after having come this far they decided to stay. They counted the total amount of money they had—$5—the price of a single admission. Only one boy could go into the house! They elected the shyest virgin in the group, slapped the $5 into his reluctant hands, and shoved him up the steps and through the door, closing it behind him.

Walking all that distance from the motel and back late at night made them very tired the next day. Coach Story never knew the secret of their misadventure. But their misadventure was not the only reason they lost to Cave-in-Rock 58-36. This outstanding team from Illinois stunned the Cubs by using the full-court zone press, a tactic that surprised even Coach Story. Howie would get the ball, throw it behind his back to change his dribble, and a Cave-in-Rock player would come up behind Howie's back on his blind side, get the ball, and lay it in. All five of the Cave-in-Rock crew were incredibly fast, and they were all over the court, baffling the disorganized Cuba team. This game was the only time the Cubs ever saw Coach Story outcoached, unable to respond to another team's tactics.

Back into the regular season play, the Cubs won over Brewers 80-41, Murray 90-40, Wingo 97-65, and Nortonville 43-35. Next they rolled over Mayfield 71-31 and took the Lowes Blue Devils 86-48. At that point, Cuba had twenty wins and one loss for the 1950–1951 season.

Because of their traveling schedule, they missed days of class work. They could not possibly keep up with their studies and did not even try. But by that time, the team was so protected by Coach Story and by the aura that surrounded them that they were no longer expected to achieve academically. For a while their teachers were conscientious about getting the most work they could from the players whenever they were in class. But in time the teachers simply gave up expecting much from the Cubs and passed them on whatever work they did so that the boys stayed eligible to play. They ignored the boys' absences.

No one believed that this behavior was right, but everyone— teachers included—accepted it. No doubt the coach and the teachers justified their actions by considering the unique experiences the boys were having traveling about the state, meeting people they would have never met, eating in fine restaurants foods they had not known existed, seeing places they might never have seen, and competing against the best teams in the state and beating them. The Cubs were getting another kind of education that may have been just as worthwhile.

Above all, a kind of joyful air of expectation prevailed all that school year; the faculty, the student body, and the community had something very unusual and very important to look forward to. Cuba—the place—had never been special before, and these boys were making Cuba really special. The whole community supported them and the school, and no one ever questioned anything Coach Story did. The basketball players, for their part, felt no loss in parting ways with formal education; they relished their fame and were thrilled with all the attention.

Although Doodle, Joe Buddy, Ted, and Paul Simpson were far more mischievous than some of the others, they all loved taking advantage of any weaknesses they saw in anyone. And they were notorious for disturbing some teachers' classes. At one point, they started wearing a popular style of flattop hats. They would take men's old hats and beat them down flat, plunk them on their heads in a rakish manner, and strut about the schoolyard. Although they were not allowed to wear hats inside the building, they would take them into class and fool with them to annoy teachers.

One young inexperienced teacher whose first name was Sunshine was particularly vulnerable. In her typing class one day, Joe Buddy and Ted decided to annoy her. Joe boldly asked Ted aloud if it was snowing. Ted answered that he did not know but would find out. Scraping his desk chair back hard as he rose, he walked to the window and said loudly, "Yep, it's snowing." Frustrated, the young teacher ordered him and Joe Buddy to go to the principal's office. The two of them smiled, put their hats on, and sauntered out of the room. The class laughed; the teacher cried.

When Coach Story met them in the hall, he asked why they were not in class. Ted answered that the teacher had kicked them out. They didn't know why; they hadn't done a thing. They had no idea what she was upset about—some women were just moody. Coach asked what he meant by that remark. Joe Buddy spoke up, agreeing with Ted that they had done nothing to disturb Sunshine; she'd been in a bad mood when class started. Coach Story stared at them for a moment, and then led them back to the classroom, where he told them and all the other typing students to go to study hall. He asked the teacher to meet with him in his office.

No one but Coach Story and the teacher knew what transpired between them that morning, but before school was out that afternoon, the teacher had tearfully apologized to Joe Buddy and Ted. As soon as the semester ended, she resigned and moved away. Certainly, Coach Story's behavior in this case is impossible to defend.

It is clear that Jack Story expected all students to do their best and to behave. But it is also clear that when it came to these boys on the basketball team, he placed far more emphasis on basketball than he did on academics. This small group had such extraordinary athletic ability and such an extraordinarily good chance to win the state championship that he did not want to sacrifice that opportunity for anything or anybody.

Jack Story knew, too, that his players would never go to college unless they had athletic scholarships. They probably would not even have graduated from high school had he not kept them involved in basketball. In those days, being successful or even simply involved in sports was a surefire way to get boys to stay in school. He must have figured that if he could get them into college, they, all intelligent boys, would have a chance to build better lives for themselves. But without basketball, they had no chance for a college education, and without that, their lives were doomed to be the same as their parents'.

22

The Season of Joy and Sorrow

If you think losing with good sportsmanship is as good as winning,
then why in the hell do they keep score?
—Adolph Rupp

Early in January 1951, the Cubs lost their second game of the season when Clark County, the number one team in the state rankings, beat them 62-61. The day the Cubs left for Winchester to play Clark County, snow was falling heavily in Kentucky. They left early that morning because Winchester was twenty miles beyond Lexington, an eight-hour drive. Needing an extra driver, Coach Story asked Jess Warren, who seldom drove far out of Graves County, to let some of the boys ride with him. Joe Buddy, Jess's son, along with Howie, Doodle, Ted, and Jimmie, piled into Jess's car on this trip. The highways were dangerously slick with ice and, as darkness fell, the roads got worse.

Just outside of Lexington, Jess noticed a slight rise in the highway and a highway sign that he could not see to read because of thickly falling snow. Thinking that he was approaching a hill, he was worried he'd get halfway up the icy road without enough power to get over the incline, so he sped forward about thirty yards. All too abruptly, he realized that they were going downhill at a break-neck speed. Much to everyone's horror, they were headed toward the narrow ice-covered bridge spanning the Kentucky River. Holding tightly to the steering wheel, trying to keep control of the car, Jess bit the stem off his pipe as his car skimmed and skidded over the frozen road and rolled onto the bridge at great speed. No one said a word until they crossed that bridge; then they all sighed with relief. Less than thirty minutes before the game was to start, they arrived in Winchester tired, cold, and still shaken. They lost to Clark County 62-61.

The Clark County game was followed by a win over Farmington, 76-45. Cuba completely outclassed Farmington, leading 18-8 at the half. Farmington's coach, W. W. Chumbler, had instructed his players to stall, to freeze the ball as early as they could to prevent Cuba from scoring. But Cuba had such a great defense that getting the ball to Howie to dribble was not difficult. And once Howie had the ball, no one could take it away from him. The Cubs got so far ahead and the game was so boring and slow, they asked Coach Story during the break if they could perform their Globetrotters act, something that they had not done thus far in any game. Thinking the audience would enjoy the performance and he would too, he told them to go ahead.

The surprised crowd went wild as the Cubs started the same way the Globetrotters start their games, by playing the four-man weave with another player set up at the post. Propelled by the fans' enthusiasm, the Cubs did all kinds of stunts; they passed the ball while pretending to read a newspaper, they acted as if they were playing baseball, and they even attempted a football field goal while poor helpless Farmington stood aghast. When the game was over, the Cubs received a standing ovation.

Their performance that night established their reputation as what the newspapers often called, after that, the most colorful high school team ever to play basketball. The Associated Press picked up the story about their act, and an article about the Cuba Cubs appeared in newspapers across the nation. Within a few days after the article appeared, Coach Story got a call from Abe Saperstein, manager of the Harlem Globetrotters, who had read the article in a St. Louis newspaper. He invited Coach Story and the Cubs to come to St. Louis as his guests for an appearance with the Globetrotters. That trip was one of the highlights of the boys' young lives. In his publicity material, Saperstein capitalized on the opportunity by inserting in the programs photographs of Doodle with Tatum, Howie with Haynes, and Coach Story with Saperstein.

After the game with Farmington, the Cubs beat Fulton 70-40 and Wingo 90-63. In the annual Mayfield Charities Invitational Game, they beat the highly ranked Lone Oak's Purple Flash 80–69. Then came victories over Symsonia 77-49, Lynn Grove 64-55, and Cayce 92-40, to end the 1951 regular season with a record of 27-2. Because of their success, the Cubs were envied and often hated by other teams in their area; name-callings and fights occurred on many occasions.

Cuba then embarked on a commanding march through the district tournament and into the regional ones. The Cubs opened the district tournament with an 86-45 defeat of Lowes. In the semifinals, they took Sedalia 62-51, and then Mayfield 74-29 in the finals, to win the district championship, extending their record to 30-2.

In the regional tournament, Cuba met Paducah Tilghman, the defending regional champion. Tilghman was tall and strong, with players destined for All-American collegiate careers in football as well as basketball. The game was memorably rough. Tilghman was determined not to lose, and its players used some unsportsmanlike tactics in guarding Cuba. Instead of their hands, they used their fingernails while grabbing for the ball, and they dug into Cuba flesh every chance they got.

Cuba built a lead and in the second half played a deliberate game, holding the ball for prolonged periods. The Cubs took only fifteen shots in the entire half and hit eight of them. Howie provided a fancy dribbling performance that left the crowd cheering and the Paducah team gasping. Jimmy Jones scored 5 points in the final three minutes of play. Tilghman players went from frustration to desperation, literally scratching and clawing to get back into the game. His uniform stained with his own blood, Doodle fouled out with two minutes to go.

Joe Buddy made his teammates laugh when he told them, "Praise the Lord! But please don't pass me that ball. I don't want to be the one who loses this game for us." And the Cubs held on. Tilghman pulled within 2 points with twenty-three seconds to go, but Cuba won 51-46. That night Coach Story did something he rarely did—he congratulated his team, saying he was proud of the boys for not responding in kind to Tilghman's ruthless attempts to get ahead.

With that victory, the stage was set for Cuba to go against Wickliffe for the regional championship. If they won this game, they would go to the state tournament. The players faced Wickliffe eagerly and enthusiastically, knowing that they had to fight all the way because Wickliffe, disappointed the previous year in the finals against Tilghman, was determined to win this time around. Wickliffe's crown prince was Phil Rollins, a handsome athlete whom sportswriters described as the classy cager. Phil was every bit the All-American that he had been rated. A junior, he was a smooth worker who rebounded on defense and sparked Wickliffe in its brilliant drive. But even Rollins could not stop Cuba that night.

Although Wickliffe quickly opened in the first minute and a half with an 8-1 lead, the Cubs got going like wildfire and ran their lead up to 22-12 in the first quarter. At one time in the second period, Cuba had a 15-point lead before Rollins made three baskets as Wickliffe cut the margin to 40-29 at halftime. Doodle was out of the game nearly all of the third period because of personal fouls but returned to the court in the fourth period, beefing Cuba's score to 51-40. Wickliffe started making a dramatic comeback when Poole, Rollins, Shockly, and Morgan rocked the Cubs as they kept springing back. Although the Blue Tigers never could overcome that lead, they furiously crept up some in the fourth quarter. Cuba was alert in rebounding and threw up a defense that Wickliffe could not penetrate. Jimmie Webb, Raymon, and Howie aided Doodle in controlling both backboards.

With only a minute and a half left in the game and Cuba leading at 62-59, Rollins drove in for a layup, tossed the ball, but missed. He was benched because of personal fouls, but he had played a good game. The leading scorer was Rollins with 25 points. In the scoring column for Cuba in that game, Doodle had 19 points, Howie 18, and Joe Buddy 2. Cuba won the game, 65-59.

The Murray State president, Dr. Ralph Woods, presented the trophies that evening. Jubilant Cuba supporters mobbed the Cubs and Coach Story, hugging and kissing them and lifting them onto their shoulders. At that moment, Graves County began planning a big sendoff for the Cubs, who were headed for the 1951 state tournament.

As already described, the Cubs lost to Clark County in the 1951 state tournament, but their disappointment vanished that same night after they swore to return the next year and win.

23

Cubs Turning into Lions

Thunder is good. Thunder is impressive; but it's lightning
that does the work.
—Mark Twain

The Cubs kept their promise about building their endurance. They ran and practiced basketball hard all summer long. People in Cuba and in Pilot Oak watched with admiration as the boys streaked across fields chasing rabbits. By January 1952, they were actually catching rabbits, some folks said. Many early mornings before school, Howie and Doodle (after his chores) ran three miles from their homes to Wray's, where Ted Bradley and Jimmie Webb lived. Then all four of them ran the four miles to Cuba and would be at school before the school bus arrived. Every afternoon they practiced in the gym. Often in the evenings they ran ten miles to Mayfield and back. And they did all this exercise without any prompting from Coach Story.

One month before basketball season began, the starters began running up and down the bleachers fifty times and around the gym sixty times a day. Then after school they ran to Harper's, two miles round trip from the school. On weekends Doodle and Howie would be seen running up and down the Murray road every morning and then playing one-on-one in Pilot Oak in front of the store. Nothing, absolutely nothing, was going to keep them from being stronger and better should they make it to the state tournament that year. They were heading toward the new basketball season with a confidence and enthusiasm that sometimes got them into trouble with their teachers—again.

Because of their disruptive behavior, Mr. Dowell refused to let them remain in his agriculture class, and he told Coach Story one morning in plain English to figure out what to do with "your boys" because he was having nothing to do with them from then on— "basketball stars or not." For the rest of the day, a grim-faced Coach Story went about his work annoyed at being put in such a difficult position. He could not send them to study hall because they needed a credit class, and there was no other class for the boys to take that period and no other teacher available to teach agriculture.

The next morning, when Coach Story passed Mrs. Sandifer, the home economics teacher, in the hall, it dawned on him that he could create a special class that she could instruct. Although Mrs. Sandifer, forty or so years old, was less than five feet tall and hardly weighed ninety pounds, she was a disciplinarian with absolute control over her classroom. She taught not only home economics but penmanship, manners, and diction as well. No one in her class dared to use such poor pronunciation as "idn'it" or "yesterdee" or "ovair thar." And no one misbehaved in her classes. Coach Story talked to her about his problem and how he wanted to solve it. Later that day, he told his wife that Mrs. Sandifer accepted the challenge as cheerfully as if she were looking forward to it.

The basketball team and a few other students were placed in this special home economics class created just for them. They were all happy, thinking little bitty Mrs. Sandifer would be easy on them, regardless of what they'd heard other kids say about her being tough.

At the first class meeting, Mrs. Sandifer presented her syllabus and told her students what she expected them to do, and how and when they were going to do it. She left no time for questions and discussion. The moment she turned her back to write on the board, Jimmie Webb, thinking she was funny looking, leaned close to Ted, giggling and whispering to him. Jimmie did not know that Mrs. Sandifer's peripheral vision was as good as, if not better than, Howie's. Surprising the thunder out of him, she reached over and vigorously yanked a thatch of his curly hair and pulled it as hard as she could several times. He thought she was going to keep pulling until she jerked his scalp off. Her actions made such a vivid impression on him that morning that neither he nor any of the others gave her any problems after that.

That class turned out to be one of the boys' best, and Mrs. Sandifer, their favorite teacher. From her they learned practical life skills: how to cook a meal, set a table, serve food, eat properly, preserve foods, make beds, tie a necktie, wash and fold clothes, iron, clean a house, mend socks, and sew on buttons. Every assignment had to meet her high standards. In addition, she taught them to write thank-you and sympathy notes and explained the importance of doing each.

The school had no classes in drama, debate, or art, no glee club or band, and it seldom sponsored formal proms or dances. Some in Cuba believed that dancing was a sin. For recreation, Doodle, Howie, Mason Harris, and Jimmie Webb formed a quartet, singing gospel music mostly, and Mary Nell Morris played the piano for them. They often practiced singing at Howie's house, where Alta Ruth, who loved music, sang along with them. Eventually they entered a Future Farmers of America talent contest in nearby Benton, Kentucky, and won second place.

Ann Dick Hainline was Cuba's Senior Basketball Queen of 1951–1952 and Jackie Saxon was Junior Basketball Queen. (Cuba school yearbook photo.)

That fall of 1951, Doodle and his friends buzzed around the county in a '36 Chevy he bought for $23 from Mutt Johnson in Cuba. He bought it with money he had earned in Detroit, where he worked for a few weeks that summer. Similar to, but even worse than, the vehicle that Jimmie had owned, this car just had a frame but no hood, no windshield, no doors, no trunk, no running board, and no lights. It was a shell of a car with only a motor, a radiator, a steering wheel, and a front and back seat. Nonetheless, the car brought them much happiness. Dressed in clean, starched shirts, blue jeans, and white touring caps that they had bought in Mayfield, they loved riding in that old heap of junk. Their girlfriends thought it was grand, too. On Saturday nights, as many boys and their dates who could cram into the car would pile in at a time, and off they would go to Mayfield to Story's Drive-In, better known as the "passion pit." (Story's had no connection to Coach Story.) Then they would drive back at night—with no car lights. Two boys held flashlights so Doodle could see the road. They did not have to worry about hitting other vehicles, though, because hardly any other automobiles were ever on the roads in Cuba or Pilot Oak at night. People in the country went to bed just after dusk. There was still no electricity in many places and nowhere to go, except to sleep.

Although Coach Story was pleased with the improvements the boys had made in their athletic skills, they often made life difficult for him. They frequently bickered among themselves, threatened to quit the team, or made some kind of trouble that he had to straighten out. Although he wanted them to be confident and proud of their achievements, he did not want to see them become what he called "biggity." And they were certainly getting that way.

At one point, after his head began "to swell," Jimmie Webb went into a slump, and Coach Story started taking him out of games and using Bill Pollock or Jimmy Brown instead. By now Jimmie and Martha Lou were married, living with his parents until school was out and he could work full-time. Wanting an income and independence, Jimmie considered quitting the team and looking for a job.

For some time he had been upset with Coach Story, mainly because Coach never let him know when he was going to use him as a starter, and he did not let Jimmie play as much anymore. Believing that he was being mistreated, Jimmie stiffened his back one morning and approached Coach Story, telling him he wanted to play more and wanted to know ahead of time if he was going to be a starter, just the same as Howie, Doodle, and Raymon always knew they were. Jimmie warned, "And if I don't get more playing time, I

When Jimmie Webb first met Martha Casey he was so shy he could barely look her in the eye. That changed, for they married before their senior year. They're shown here the day after their graduation from Cuba. (Photo courtesy of Jimmie Webb.)

am going to quit the team and leave school." Coach Story replied matter-of-factly, "Well, Webb, you just go ahead and quit." Turning away quickly, he looked back and added, "But you can be cocksure that I'll draw my paycheck just the same." Jimmie decided to remain on the team.

Coach Story had another serious headache after all the starters played hooky one day. That incident created a ruckus in the whole community, not just at school. According to the school policy, if, for whatever reason, a student did not show up in the morning, there was no problem; he was simply counted as absent. If he came in at noon, he would be counted absent for a half day. But if he ever left the school grounds after he had arrived, he was in big trouble. Leaving without permission was, in Coach Story's mind, equivalent to a felony.

After the Cubs returned from a ten-day trip traveling from Mayfield to Maysville, at the opposite end of the state, playing nine

Jack Story. (Photo courtesy of Barbara Story Crowell.)

games in ten days in different towns and cities, they needed hair-cuts and rest badly. Coach Story hated seeing long hair on a male, no matter his age. Knowing that fact, Doodle one morning asked him if they all could go to Mayfield to get haircuts and then come directly back to school. Coach Story did not want them to miss any more classes, but he did want them to look good for the next game, which was coming up soon. He told them if they promised to hurry back and not stop anyplace else, they could go. Off they merrily went.

It was one of those summerlike autumn mornings—cool, clear, and beautiful. The boys were in an especially joyful mood. The semester was nearly over; the Christmas holidays and the invi-tational, district, and regional tournaments were coming up soon. And then there would be the state tournament in March—just wait-ing for them to arrive! They had so much to look forward to. After getting their haircuts, which hardly took any time at all, they figured they had a few extra minutes to stop by the pool hall. They thought that by now, with all of their accomplishments, Coach Story and the teachers would not care so much if they were a little late. After all, they were seniors and graduating that spring, and they were going to be the 1952 state champions. Besides, they thought that as long as they got back by noon for ball practice, Coach Story might not even miss them.

More mature than the others, Raymon, nearly twenty, had also just married. He exerted a big-brother influence, always trying to keep the rest of them out of trouble. He never wanted to make Coach Story angry. He had done that once in the ninth grade and never forgot the paddling Coach gave him. So Raymon urged the others to return to school immediately. Howie was inclined to agree with him but decided to stay. Doodle assured them that Coach Story was not going to paddle any of them; they were too old for that kind of thing now. And they were too important to the team. If Coach did anything at all, Joe Buddy argued, he would give them three days' suspension. Upon hearing that, Ted chirped cheerily that that would be swell and urged Raymon to go along with them. Ted told Raymon, "We're nineteen years old. Why, hell, man, you're twenty and married! He won't paddle a *married* man!" Unconvinced, Raymon left, saying he would see them at practice after lunch.

Later that morning, Coach Story rounded the corners of the school building looking for his team. When he couldn't find his players, he sent Jess Warren (Joe Buddy's dad) to search for them. By then the whole high school student body knew that the starters had skipped, and they were giggling with glee thinking about the repercussions that soon would follow.

Jess found the boys in Watson's Pool Room in Mayfield. The moment they saw him walk in, their spirits fell. The drive back to Cuba was a silent one. When they got in sight of the school, they saw a clench-jawed Coach Story planted solidly in front of the building, waiting for them. With a stern expression on his face, he stared at them as they got out of the car and started toward him. It was a day none of them would ever forget. In a throaty voice, Coach Story said, "Get dressed for practice and go to my office." Joe Buddy flinched and stuttered, "But, Mr. Story, sir, we just went to get a haircut, sir, and it took longer than we thought it would, sir." They could see his anger deepening, and his stare sent shivers through them.

His office was no larger than eight by ten feet, and his desk and three wooden straight-back chairs took up most of the room. Yet the somber group crammed into it. A few awards, pictures of his wife and children, and his bachelor's degree from Murray were hanging crookedly on the walls. In the corner near the door was a metal coat rack piled with a couple of his old jackets and his straw hat. In another corner on the floor were his mud-caked work boots and a pair of worn-out basketball shoes. Textbooks and papers littered his desk. The wall behind the desk was lined with bookshelves, stacked mostly with textbooks, annuals, telephone books, sports books and magazines, and some newspapers. He had taped to that wall a few quotations he wanted to save. The one window was wide and half-way covered with a faded white shade.

But the only thing the boys noticed was the large wooden paddle lying on his desk. This principal's paddle was about twenty-eight inches long and three-quarters of an inch thick. It was one that Coach Story had made himself out of hickory wood. It angled nar-rowly down on one end to provide his hand a good grip; the other end widened out to twelve inches across. The most mysterious thing was how he managed to hide that paddle from everyone, including his friend Jess Warren, who helped him out at school. Its location had to be kept secret or else some boy would surely have stolen it and thrown it into the huge potbellied stove that heated the gym.

Facing Coach Story, the boys stood erect, hands clasped behind their backs and feet spread apart. Coach leaned back in his chair, crossed his legs, and folded his arms over his chest. He stared at them for what seemed like a long time. Then he reached over to the right side of his desk and flicked on the switch to the newly installed intercom system, which permitted the entire high school faculty and student body to hear what was going on in his office. Knowing this embarrassed the boys, Coach Story began, "Well, now, according to the school policy for skipping school, you have the option of a three-day suspension or five licks with this paddle."

Sighing with relief that the five licks were not going to be an automatic punishment, Joe Buddy spoke first, saying that he would take the suspension. "I don't think so," Coach Story replied coldly. "I think you and the others *prefer* the five licks." His words sent pangs of fear and made them dizzy. With games coming up soon, Coach was not about to let them lose three days of practice, or let them get away without paying for their little escapade either.

Without any further discussion, he stood, took off his coat, unbuttoned his collar, and loosened his tie as the boys exchanged horrified glances. He opened the door and instructed them to wait outside and line up in alphabetical order. "Bradley, you're first. Stay here!" he ordered. "The rest of you wait outside."

Jess Warren waited anxiously with them. Jimmie recalled, "We were wearing just our T-shirts and practice trunks and had nothing to block the blows. Coach Story had us bend over his desk so he could whack us hard. And he did! The pain was terrible. He was a strong man. His hands were like bear paws, and he could swing that paddle. He blistered our rear ends that day. It was an humiliating experience, too."

They didn't want the student body to hear them groan, so they took their licks as silently as possible. However, Jess Warren sobbed loudly and shed big tears while his son Joe Buddy was taking his punishment. The other students, of course, thought this event was hilarious; as always, kids love to see other kids get their comeuppance.

After Coach Story finished doling out his punishment, he followed the silent boys into the gym for the regular afternoon practice. Feeling superior to the others for not staying in Mayfield, Raymon confidently walked into the gym, carrying under his arm his little green satchel containing his practice outfit and shoes. When Coach Story spotted him, he mistakenly thought that Raymon had sneaked into school and had hid until now. Coach Story angrily refused to listen to Raymon's explanation and ordered him to his office.

The other boys sat on the bleachers, suspecting what was about to happen, as they watched Raymon follow Coach Story. A few short minutes later, Raymon walked back into the gym, stepping gingerly, his little green satchel still tucked under his arm. His rear end felt as if it had been stung by hundreds of wasps, his face was beet red, and his eyes were bugged out. He exuded anger. When the others saw his facial expression up close, they doubled over with laughter, and that made him even angrier. "Every damn one of you go to hell and stay there!" he growled.

24

Lexington, Here We Come!

All things are won by diligence.
—Menander

During their senior year, the Cubs paid little attention to their schoolwork. It was impossible to keep up with it, tutors or no tutors. Wanting the players to have all the experience they could, Coach Story completely revised their schedule, so that they played one game after another. In addition to playing all the area schools in Graves County, they played in every invitational tournament in the state, plus many charity games. They played the top teams in the state and also the number one and number two teams in Tennessee.

They opened the 1951–1952 season with four quick wins: over Wingo, 82-36; Farmington, 72-34; Fancy Farm, 120-18; and Columbia, 76-50. Next they traveled to Maysville, in northern Kentucky, clear across the state, where they won the Burley Invitational Tobacco Bowl Tournament by beating Carrolton 60-43 in the opening round, and Inez 75-52 for the championship. Doodle was in complete control of his shooting and rebounding in this tournament, and he played defense superbly. In the Carrolton game, he was the leading scorer with 27 points, followed by Howie with 13, Bill Pollock with 6, and Raymon and Jimmie with 4 each; Harold Roberts contributed 3, and Joe Buddy added 2.

In the championship game against Inez, the Cubs played a splendid floor game and controlled the backboards just as they had done with Carrolton. During this game, Doodle's performance was what the local sportswriters described as "spectacular." Having never seen the boy's hook shot, they were immensely impressed with his technique, a unique windmill that connected repeatedly. Doodle led all the scorers with 29 points, helping the Cubs forge ahead at the outset of the second period.

Shooting from the perimeter and driving to the basket, Howie collected 17 points of his own. He put the Cubs ahead by 15 during the second half with a quick behind-the-back dribble around the man guarding him followed by a speedy drive to the basket for an uncontested layup. Jimmie contributed 13 points in the Inez game, Joe Buddy 6, Bill Pollock 4, and Raymon and Paul Simpson 2 each.

The Cubs returned to the regular season schedule and kept winning. Their victories included wins over Saint Mary's, 64-41; Metropolis, Illinois, 54-47; Lowes, 92-36; Brewers, 74-60; Symsonia, 86-56; and Henderson's Holy Name, 47-30, improving their 1951–1952 record to 12-0. Next they won the Paducah Invitational Christmas Championship Tournament by defeating Crittenden County 86-48, Bandana 70-61, and the highly regarded Lone Oak 72-54.

Beating Lone Oak was especially sweet. Coached by Don Stephenson, Lone Oak had an excellent ball club that year. Sonny Hubbs, "Slick" Herndon, Tommy Stephenson, and six-foot-seven Ken Donaldson were all outstanding players, but that night they were no match for Cuba. Doodle, recovering from the flu, scored only 9 points, but Howie led with 27 and Joe Buddy added 12.

The night they played the Brewers game was a good example of Coach Story's flexibility. For some reason (probably because of their overpowering sense of superiority at that point), the Cubs decided they were not going to dribble the ball the first half, and they did not. The ball did not touch the floor; they just passed it. Although they were just barely ahead, Coach Story remained silent. They won the game but not by as many points as they could and should have.

After they whipped Lowes 116-49 for their sixteenth straight victory, they proceeded to the Purchase-Pennyrile Basketball Tournament at Murray. In the first game, Wickliffe handed Cuba its first loss of the season, 52-51. The Cubs chalked their defeat up to bad luck: Raymon, with sore ankles, was not up to speed, and Howie and Jimmy Webb were suffering from the flu. The Cubs then played Henderson's Holy Name in the consolation game, winning 71-56.

The regular season schedule picked up again with the Cubs coming out ahead of Sedalia 59-41. That Friday they traveled the long trip to Lexington, where they again lost, 48-41, to Louisville Manual, one of the largest schools in the state. In that game Doodle badly injured his already sore ankle and scored only 5 points. He sat out the entire third quarter. Trying to take up the slack, Howie scored 20 points, the only Cub to reach double digits. With Howie guarding him, Phil Grawmeyer, Manual's All-State center and leading scorer, was able to make only 10 points that game, and it was Curtis Moffett, with 16, who led Manual to victory.

The next morning the Cubs went on to Horse Cave to play Caverna, another top-notch team. Even though Raymon had a nasty cold and Doodle, with a swollen ankle, was barely able to play part of the half, the Cubs inched passed Caverna 36-31, proving how tough they were.

After playing eight games in nine days, Cuba was scheduled to meet Selmer, Tennessee's number one team, in the Fifteenth Annual Mayfield Charities Invitational Tournament. Every contest Cuba played in western Kentucky was a sellout game. However, this one on Monday night, January 21, 1952, featuring undefeated Selmer and Cuba, created such a demand for tickets that Mayfield's fire marshal canceled his plans to have two games played that night. Only 1,750 people could be seated in the gym, and the fire marshal had been beset with requests from frustrated, angry people who wanted in. After 1,750 tickets had been sold, the gate closed. The fire marshal said that 5,000 tickets could easily have been sold for that game alone.

Several hundred supporters from the little Tennessee community of Selmer accompanied their team to Mayfield, but Cuba supporters outnumbered them. Among those attending that night was Coach Ed Diddle. The Tennessee newspapers, promoting the game as a charity benefit, announced, "The Lions should provide Jack Story's quintet with a real test—as they feature a fast break attack combined with speed and lots of rebound power." Coached by Jerry Smith, a graduate of Lambuth College in Jackson, Tennessee, Selmer's Lions had a reputation for being extremely aggressive and speedy. With a string of fifty-three consecutive victories, Selmer was banking on an undefeated season that year.

Jack Story was jittery the night of the game. He knew that the Lions resembled the Cave-in-Rock quintet that had surprised him the year before and beat his team in the Paducah Invitational Tournament. He wanted badly to beat Selmer because Selmer was so highly rated, but feared his boys might not be physically able to win that night. He had been pressing them too hard in the past two weeks. They had traveled the long trip to Lexington Friday and then on to Horse Cave the following night. Raymon was still sick, and Doodle's bluish-black ankle was swollen to the size of a grapefruit. Coach Story knew that there was no way Doodle could play at 100 percent in the Selmer game, but he was going to start with him. He hoped that Howie could carry the extra-heavy load that night.

Selmer scouted Cuba and saw for itself what the newspapers had been hailing as "Cuba's scoring twins." So when Selmer faced Cuba that night, its players doubled up on Howie and Doodle, leaving Jimmie Webb, Joe Buddy, and Bill Pollock nearly open. Taking advantage of the situation, Joe Buddy connected early in the game with a set shot from twenty-five feet, and from that moment on, the Cubs were in charge all the way. Jimmie Webb scored 15 points in the first half and by halftime the lead was Cuba's, 40-23.

In disbelief and despair, Selmer fans sat tearfully wringing their hands as they watched the Cubs collect their twentieth victory of the season against two losses, 69-50. Despite his sore ankle, Doodle kept capturing the ball as it bounced off the boards while Selmer players swarmed around him. In offense, Doodle made brilliant windmill shots from all sections of the court and racked up a total of 24 points. Jimmie ripped the nets on set shots and scored 19 points total. Howie also made 19 points, all in the last half. Joe Buddy added 4 buckets and Raymon 3. Both Joe and Raymon put in good performances in the first half, but Joe fouled out early in the second half. Raymon, with four personal fouls, sat on the bench much of the time. Bill, Harold, Ted, and Jimmy Brown came through supportively. The Lions could not penetrate Cuba's defense, and the Cubs moved to an easy victory. In the closing ceremony that night, Ed Diddle, accompanied by Kelly Thompson, assistant to the president at Western Kentucky University in Bowling Green, presented a handsome trophy to Coach Story.

Returning to the regular season action, Cuba won over Symsonia 58-42 on January 22, and the following night beat Warren County 64-38. Next was the Louisville Invitational Tournament, where the Cubs beat Louisville Male 63-50 and Campbellsville 48-44, only to lose to Louisville Manual in the finals 70-58, for their third loss of the season. By this time Raymon's cold had spread to Howie and Jimmie Webb, and Doodle's ankle was still swollen and sore. With four starters disabled, it was no surprise they lost again at Allen County, 49-48.

Despite their health problems, the Cubs redeemed themselves for an earlier loss by beating Wickliffe 68-33, but Wickliffe was playing without its star player Phil Rollins, who had been injured. The Cubs next played Humbolt, Tennessee, and won 74-52, but then lost to Clark County 57-48. The final game of the 1952 regular season ended with their win, again, over Lone Oak, 67-62. They entered the state tournament play with a record of 27-5. The Cubs won the district tournament by defeating Farmington 70-35, Wingo 88-58, and Symsonia 67-36.

In the opening game of the 1952 regional tournament, Cuba ran over Clinton 74-29, and then whipped Symsonia in the semifinals 61-34 to advance to the finals against Wickliffe. They played a great defensive game and defeated Wickliffe 54-42, even with a healthy Phil Rollins back in the lineup. With their victory over Wickliffe, the Cubs had again earned a ticket to the state tournament. Although his ankle was still sore, Doodle did not slow down. He led the scoring against Wickliffe with 24 points, making eight field goals in the second half, most of them coming from his trademark windmill shots. As usual, Howie stunned the crowd with his fancy ball-handling act and added 14 points. Jimmie Webb added 8 more.

Unlike the 1950–1951 season, this season had been a real struggle. As seniors, the boys had suffered many injuries and illnesses. Still, even though they had lost their floor general Jimmy Jones, who had graduated the previous May, they'd gained Bill Pollock, a definite asset, as well as Jimmy Brown, a great substitute center, and Harold Roberts, a strong forward. Their victories had always been team victories and always would be. The Cuba Cubs advanced to the 1952 state tournament with a 33-5 record.

Kentucky basketball fans watched with a heightened sense of anticipation.

25

The Little Comeback Team

Of all human powers operating on the affairs of mankind, none is
greater than that of competition.
—Henry Clay

On Wednesday, March 19, 1952, the day the tournament was to
begin, *Lexington Herald-Leader* sportswriter Larry Shropshire
reminded readers in his column "Down in Front" of the criticism
out-of-town teams and their fans and other visitors had heaped on
Lexington (the host of the state tournament) the previous year. He
expressed hope that criticism could be avoided this year and from
now on. Then he explained the reason for the criticism:

The colorful team from distant Cuba . . . was inadvertently and
unintentionally the hub of the trouble with certainly no blame
whatsoever to be attached to those lads. Catching the fancy of
the crowd on their first trip to the state meet, the Cubs suddenly and quite unexpectedly, no doubt, acquired a tremendous and very noisy rooting section. They could do no wrong,

in the eyes of the tourney throngs, and their opponents could do no right, or at least nothing to receive the approval of the noisy majority of the onlookers. Cuba picked up more well-wishers and more vocal support than any other team competing in a Kentucky tournament ever had, and that surely was all right until the cheering for the Cubs reached the point where it was almost fanatical—much to the distress and pained concern of players and supporters of the opposing team.

Not only were the loud cheers for the favorites offensive, but also the boos and yells at officials whenever they made calls against the Cubs. Cuba rooters were rude and hurt the feelings of players on the other teams. Feelings reached the point where the tourney crowd even strongly opposed the local entry, University High, in its game with Cuba. . . . Such rabid partisanship displayed by some tourney crowds last year should be avoided this time around.

Shropshire's advice, however, went unheeded. When the Cubs returned to Lexington in 1952, fans crammed into Memorial Coliseum to give them a hero's welcome. The press also gave them a warm welcome, agreeing with Jack Anderson, the editor of the *Sun-Democrat,* who wrote, "No University of Kentucky basketball team ever got the reception in the Coliseum that the Cubs got Friday and Saturday nights."

In the opening game of the tournament, the Cubs went up against Corbin, rated stronger than any of the other teams Cuba had defeated at the state tournament the year before. Corbin's Red Hounds were powered by Jerry Bird, a big center whom many described as the best college prospect in the state.

At the start, it looked as if this might be a close game all the way. The teams traded baskets through four early ties before the Red Hounds moved out to an 18-14 lead after one quarter—on the strength of Bird's 13 points. The Cubs tried everything to control Corbin's center, but with little success. It was beginning to look as if he might whip them single-handedly.

With three quarters to go, Coach Story knew that he had to change Cuba's defensive tactics; the original plan wasn't working. The team had to interfere more with Bird's ability to score, so he switched guards. He had the much shorter Howie guard six-foot-seven Bird, instructing Howie "to run around him like a guinea after corn!" He told Doodle to be alert: when Corbin tried to lob the ball over Howie, Doodle was to sag back and help guard Bird.

Howie did exactly what Coach Story wanted him to do. He circled Bird, sometimes in front, sometimes on the sides. He kept right on him and was quick enough to knock the ball away from Bird when one of the Corbin players attempted to pass the ball to the center. Many times Howie was able to slap the ball so that one of the Cubs could get it. Cuba would not have scored enough to beat Corbin if Bird had been allowed to get the ball and go to the basket with it. But Cuba successfully kept Corbin from getting enough points to win.

Cuba's go-to guy in the first half turned out to be Jimmie Webb. Behind Jimmie's six of six shooting from the field, the Cubs stayed within striking distance in the first half. Although Corbin led by as many as 7 points in the second quarter, Cuba closed the gap to 34-32 at intermission. It was anybody's game at that point because the Cubs had finally managed to slow down Bird, holding him to 2 second-quarter points.

As had become their trademark over the last two seasons, the Cubs still trailed well into the second half. Corbin held the edge pretty steadily because of its superiority on the boards. With Corbin still ahead 47-42 entering the fourth quarter, the big question for Cuba was Doodle. Saddled with two fouls less than a minute into the game, he had not been his usual aggressive self, choosing instead to play a cautious defense to avoid risking any further foul trouble. But time was running out on the Cubs. After Joe Buddy hit a crip shot, making the score 47-44, he then missed a pair of free throws that could have cut Corbin's lead to 1 early in the fourth quarter.

Doodle took over and again played with typical abandon. He hit with a one-handed shot that put Cuba within 1 point of Corbin. That was only the beginning. Doodle then hit a wide hook shot, with several Corbin players hanging on him. Two more Doodle-hook-shots later, Cuba was in the lead, 52-49, and there were just a little more than four minutes left in the game.

With Doodle breaking loose for the basket and being fed the ball by Howie's pinpoint passing, the score rose to 58-51 in the last two minutes. Using his hook shot, Doodle hit *six straight baskets,* scoring 12 of his 22 points in the last quarter. Joe Buddy added 2 points for good measure. As Cuba pulled away for a 60-53 victory, with Howie killing the clock with more of his dazzling dribbling, the Coliseum crowd went wild with joy. What a game! The Cubs had come from behind again, just as they had done the year before in games against Covington, Lexington University High, and Whitesburg. The excitement that those kinds of wins generate in basketball fans is unforgettable.

Cuba's next opponent, a night later, was Henry Clay of Lexington, a team that had advanced to the quarterfinals with a victory over College High, 62-52. For a change Cuba found a way to win without falling behind for most of the game. After Henry Clay's star guard "Sugar" Anderson scored the game's first points, the Cubs quickly came back to take an early lead and stayed in front the rest of the way. Although Henry Clay came within 3 points several times during the first quarter, it could not stop Cuba's offensive play. With Doodle's 10 points, Cuba led at the end of the first period 16-11.

In the second quarter, Cuba increased its lead to 23-13 thanks to Joe Buddy's two jump shots and Jimmie Webb's 3-point play off

Howie was a great ball handler who wasn't afraid of taking it to the hoop, either, as he does here in a 1952 state tournament game against Henry Clay. (*Lexington Herald-Leader* photo courtesy of Howard Crittenden.)

an offensive rebound. The Cubs stayed in front anywhere from 8 to 11 points the rest of the quarter and ended the half ahead 36-26.

There had even been some time for comic relief. At one point in the second quarter, Doodle split his pants, called a timeout, and rushed to the dressing room. When he returned, strutting out in a new pair of shorts, the crowd broke out into laughter.

But Cuba's laughter was short-lived. Before the half was over, Jimmie Webb had fouled out, and Raymon, one of Cuba's best rebounding hopes, had been forced to the bench with a twisted ankle. With more than a half still to play, Coach Story had to use his bench more than usual, although Bill Pollock and Harold Roberts performed admirably well in replacing Jimmie Webb and Raymon, respectively.

During the third quarter, the Blue Devils started to rally and cut Cuba's lead to 7 points, but Howie made several baskets to get the lead back into double digits, 40-29. Scrappy Henry Clay fought hard and pruned the margin to 4 points but could not do anything with Cuba's offensive play. Moving in and taking control, Doodle made two hook shots with two minutes left in the quarter, and Cuba had a 46-41 lead. Shooting one basket after another, Anderson and Duff put Henry Clay within 2 points, but then Doodle took charge and made a free throw and Howie made a tip-in. The period ended with Cuba ahead 49-44.

Early in the fourth quarter, Howie dribbled right through the entire Lexington team for a layup. Doodle drove in for a shot, and Raymon, back in the game though his ankle was sore, hit a set shot, to up the lead to 55-44. Cuba went into a semistall for the remainder of the game. Henry Clay fouled in several attempts to get the ball back, but Cuba refused the free-throw attempts and opted to keep possession of the ball. The Cubs' victory over Henry Clay, 62-47, moved them into the semifinals, where they would play Hindman on Saturday.

Because the majority of those attending the games, including many of those from Lexington, were enthusiastically rooting for Cuba, the few cheering for Henry Clay could barely be seen or heard. In an article two days earlier, the *Lexington Herald-Leader*'s

A prominent newspaper story missed the point when it labeled Howie a "show-off" for his excellent ball-handling abilities. He was a rare breed of high school basketball player who could kill lots of clock and control games in the spirit of the rules at the time. (*Lexington Herald-Leader* photo courtesy of Howard Crittenden.)

sportswriter Larry Shropshire had pointed out to his readers that such "rabid support" for one team was "hurtful," and that teams opposing Cuba were made to feel as if they "were guilty of some heinous crime. And officials making a call against Cuba were booed practically off the court." During the 1951 state tournament, the supporters of other teams were understandably hurt about the treatment they received and doubted aloud if Lexington was the right place to hold the competitions. Sportswriter Bob Adair wondered too.

The day before the final 1952 games were to be played, the disgruntled Shropshire wrote a column that indicated his attitude toward Cuba had soured, and he especially directed his wrath at Howie. "Spend just a little time on the sidelines at the Crittenden Circus—that's what the state high school tournament will have to be called as long as Cuba's Howie Crittenden is participating, the master ball handler being a super-show-off as well as relegating everything else save his own performance to the category of side-show attractions—and it becomes obvious that one change in the rule would make basketball a 100 percent better game. Stop these silly and almost continual marches from one foul line to the other while actual competition is held up."

When someone showed Shropshire's article to Howie, the boy was devastated. While playing his heart out during the games, he was tired and suffering from a toothache. He felt bad enough without learning what had been written in the newspaper about him. Trying to console him, his teammates urged him to ignore the remarks. Doodle growled, "Don't you give a rat's tail for what that pissant writes."

Many tournament regulars wrote to the paper responding to Shropshire's article, saying much the same as Oliver Wagoner Jr. said in his letter, which is worth quoting at length here:

If Crittenden is such a show-off and cannot play ball, why doesn't some of the "good" ball teams show up? Crittenden, "The Show-Off," did fairly well against Henry Clay, and I didn't see Anderson, or any of the other players on this "better" team taking the ball away from him.

I have no gripe against the teams, it is just their self-assigned defenders. When Cuba first came to the tournament last year, they were given a big write-up about where they were from and their watching the Harlem Globetrotters' films, copying their style of play from them. This was for the public and they ate it up. From then on everyone backed Cuba to the hilt, even in defeat they were great. Then Cuba beat a Lexington team, brother, that was all as far as the Lexington papers were concerned. When you say fans should support the "local" team in the tournament you are talking through your hat. A state tournament has no local team. The team and the fans come from all over the state and the fans come to see and support the teams of their choice. Also, who are you to tell all these fans that they shouldn't give Cuba their support, which they so justly deserve and, to put it bluntly, yell for whomever they damn please.

Jack Anderson, for the *Paducah Sun-Democrat,* pointed out that Shropshire was alone in lambasting Howie:

[One] hundred or more sports writers and radio announcers covering the tournament voted Crittenden the best player in the meet. . . . Now maybe we're all wrong and Mr. Shropshire is right. . . . Maybe Ed Diddle, Harlan Hodges, and several more big name coaches are all wet, too. . . . All they'd give for Crittenden's services would be their eye teeth. . . . Howie Crittenden is a great basketball player, a modest youth with a burning desire to win, and a gentleman. . . . With all respect to Doodle, Raymon, Joe, and Jimmie, the Cubs could not have won without the services of Crittenden. The youngster broke into tears when he read the slurring remarks hurled at him by the Lexington sports writer, who chose to take his wrath out on a youngster fighting his heart out to bring glory to his TEAM, not himself.

After all that excitement Friday night, Doodle was up late, standing in front of the tall window in his and Howie's hotel room looking out over the city. Jimmie Webb and Raymon, also sharing the room, were already in bed asleep. An exhausted Howie whispered, "Doodle, you got to go to sleep. We got to play tomorrow." Doodle answered, "I can't, Howie. I'm as wide awake as a turkey on a turkey shoot."

Hindman's Yellow Jackets were called the battling babies because theirs was a young mountain team without seniors. The team consisted of Garnard Martin, Willard Holiday, Jack Waddell, Fred Campbell, Gerald Engle, Archie Combs, Wayne Conley, Vernon Conley, Jennings Martin, and John Waddell. They were under terrific pressure, for it was impossible for them to ignore the crowd's support for Cuba.

In the opening moments of the semifinal game, Doodle, relaxed and happy, delighted fans and disarmed the Hindman players and their rooters by shouting, "Praise the Lord! And pass me that ball!" The crowd laughed, knowing that he was playing on the words of a popular World War II song, "Praise the Lord and Pass the Ammunition!" Doodle pointed to a spot on the floor from where he planned to shoot and score. The crowd loved it. But clenched-jawed Hindman players were not in a joking mood and showed they were ready for the fight of their lives.

That game turned out to be one of the most excruciatingly even contests in the history of the state tournament. Some spectators got so nervous that they could not watch the game anymore and left the bleachers to wait outside. Martha Casey Webb was sitting with her sister Helen and Helen's husband, Herschel Floyd. Unable to watch his baby brother on the court, Herschel buried his face in his hands and pressed his thumbs over his ears. At one point he turned his back to the game. Finally he stood up and told Helen, "I just can't stand it any longer. I've got to get out of here," and he left the stadium. Helen stayed with Martha but hid her face with her scarf.

The Cubs' biggest lead in the first quarter was only 4 points, and their lead at the end of the quarter was 11-8. At halftime, the teams were tied 19-19.

The third quarter was a thriller. Cuba took some short leads for the first four minutes, but then Hindman moved out ahead 29-28 when Garnard Martin made another basket from the circle. With thirty-five seconds to go, Jimmie Webb put Cuba ahead 34-33. But the quarter ended with a 37-37 tie, and it was nip and tuck after that. In the fourth quarter, Jimmie Webb scored a basket and Joe Buddy a free throw. The Cubs went into a stall, letting Howie dribble for two minutes while Garnard Martin and Vernon Conley chased him. With three minutes and thirty seconds to go, Doodle made a windmill shot to put Cuba up 42-37. But Garnard Martin brought Hindman back, netting a free throw and then stealing the ball from Howie for a layup that made it 42-40.

As Cuba was trying to stall, Martin again got the ball with one minute, nineteen seconds remaining and passed it to Wayne Conley, who missed his shot and a jump ball resulted. The ball was tipped to Howie, who threw it away on a long pass. Joe Buddy then fouled Garnard Martin with fifty-one seconds left. Instead of taking the ball out, Hindman let Martin shoot his foul shots: he made both, tying the game 42-42. Both teams had chances to score with the seconds ticking away in the fourth quarter, but neither could convert. Joe Buddy's last-second shot from ten feet behind the circle hit the rim and bounced off. Overtime!

Hindman and Cuba squared off for a showdown in one of the most spine-tingling contests that ever took place in the Coliseum. They did not play just one sudden-death overtime; they played two. No one scored in the first, three-minute one. Doodle shot once and missed, and so did the Yellow Jackets' Willard Holiday. Most of the time was used up with Howie's dribbling the ball. In the second sudden-death overtime, Jimmie Webb got the tip and passed the ball to Howie, who feinted and dribbled out around the foul circle

Doodle hung on the basket and the team celebrated around him after Cuba beat Louisville Manual in the 1952 championship game.

and rifled it to Doodle, standing near the baseline about fifteen feet from the basket.

In the most dramatic moment of the tournament, Doodle—holding the ball in his widespread large hand with his arm extended—leaned far and low to the right, using that position that signaled the start of his windmill shot. Sitting on the bench on either side of Coach Story were Mason Harris and Bobby McClain, student managers. Both heard Coach Story groan as he crunched over with arms folded across his stomach as if he were having cramps, mumbling, "Oh, no, no! Oh, no, no, Doodle . . . No, not now."

But Doodle was not afraid. In his mind's eye he was back in Pilot Oak in front of the store, making his perfect windmill hook shot with his *imaginary* ball. When Doodle pitched the basketball that night, it arced perfectly, sailed at least fifteen feet through the air, and sank through the hoop, dropping down cleanly, hitting nothing but the net—just as he had imagined it would. The horn blew. The stadium went berserk. Cuba had scratched out an amazing 44-42 victory.

Working his way through the crowd to where Doodle was being mobbed by fans, a red-faced Coach Story shouted, "Doodle! Don't you realize we could have lost the game if you had missed from there?" Struggling to stay upright as fans juggled him onto their shoulders, his face glistening with sweat and happiness, his eyes filled with tears, Doodle smiled and shouted back: "But Coach, I didn't *aim* to miss!"

26

A Memorable Year: 1952

Open the gates and give the victors their way.
—Shakespeare

With no time for a much-needed rest after two overtimes, the Cubs prepared themselves for the championship game that evening against Louisville Manual, which had just survived a grueling semi-final game of its own to upset Clark County 54-53. Clark County and Manual were rated first and second, respectively, in the Associated Press poll that year. Earlier, Clark County had beaten Cuba 57-48. Manual had beaten Cuba twice: the first time 48-41, and then again by 70-58 in the final game of the Louisville Invitational Tournament.

One of the largest schools in the state, if not the largest, Manual had the tallest players in the tournament. Its stars—six-foot-eight Phil "Cookie" Grawmeyer and six-foot-seven Curtis Moffett, looked like professional players. The average height of Manual's other players was six feet four, making its smallest players the same size as

Doodle, the tallest Cub. Many sports broadcasters were saying that Cuba was about to meet its nemesis in favored Manual. One radio sportscaster flatly stated that Cuba did not stand a chance against the Crimson Tide. Manual had reason to be confident it would beat Cuba a third time in the championship game, set for 8:45 p.m.

At dusk that Saturday, when the Cubs came out of the hotel to board the bus for their final ride to Memorial Coliseum, they were surprised to see the Manual team already seated on the bus. The usual procedure was for competing teams to ride in separate buses, but not on this night, for some unexplained reason.

As the Cubs lined up in front of the bus, Manual fans ran over to them. Inspired by the media hype about one man in Cuba staying home to milk all the cows while everyone else went to Lexington, some Manual fans started ringing cowbells and spewing nasty insults, calling the Cubs skinny little hicks . . . show-offs . . . hot dogs. Some shouted such comments as, "Hey, Cuba, wipe the cow manure off your shoes!" "Go on home and feed your hogs!" "Did you have corn pone and taters for supper?" Some boys were bragging that the Crimsons were going to mop up the floor that night with the little hot-doggy hicks.

As they boarded the bus, the Cubs did just what Coach Story had always told them to do—ignore insults, do not look at the speakers, and remain silent. The Manual players did not say anything either. Everyone on the bus was silent.

This trip to Lexington had made the Cubs more sensitive about their humble rural background. The city had a way of driving the idea of inferiority home to them fast. Confronting some of these city kids' swaggering sense of superiority was more than the Cubs needed to deal with at that moment. They were tired and tense, and they were facing something bigger than a game. For five years they had been close friends and teammates, living and playing together, dreaming together of winning this state championship. Now all of that was coming to an end. Not far ahead lay graduation, and the separate paths they would take into adulthood. This game was the last game they would ever play together; it marked the end of their boyhood together.

As the bus drove through the narrow streets to the Coliseum, the Cubs were quiet and tense. The streetlights and flickering neon signs they passed illuminated the serious expressions on their handsome young faces. They were country kids in the city, and to be called so was humiliating—in 1952 a pejorative distinction was made between *city* people and *country* people. And no matter how many games they won, they were still *country*. When that fact was pointed out to them in such a mean manner, it hurt, but it also hardened them and made them all the more determined to win that night.

In previous dark times, their sense of humor had pulled them through, and it did again on that bus ride. It was not Doodle this time who brightened the scene; it was Robert Peters, one of their team's managers. Never an athlete, Peters had always wanted to be an evangelical preacher, and he never missed an opportunity to preach. A few months earlier, one of his neighbors had given him her late husband's Sunday suit, shirt, and tie. Her husband had been a Baptist minister, and Peters felt inspired to preach whenever he wore this outfit. In fact, Peters had taken to dressing up in it and standing outside the school preaching several mornings a month as the children arrived.

That night Peters was so upset with the Manual fans' ugly behavior that he jumped out of his seat and ran to the front of the bus. Consumed with sincere zeal, he whipped out a frayed Bible from his back pocket, and with power and conviction began pointing and shouting at the Manual players, who sat in shocked astonishment. "*Sinners! Repent your wicked ways. This is the end for you! Your time has come.*" His eyes bulged, and his Adam's apple bobbed like a yo-yo as he brandished the Bible and quoted scripture. The

As intense as the Cubs were on the court, this photo of student manager Bobby McClain shows that student support off the court went even a notch higher. (Cuba school yearbook photo.)

Cubs grinned as Peters, glaring at the Manual players, continued his tirade.

The Manual team did not think Peters was amusing, but his own team did. He had diluted some of the Cubs' tension. The Cubs knew their time had come too, and they were ready. They were going into the game as relaxed as possible, and they were going to win.

At the Coliseum that night, when it came time for the two teams to face each other, the organist played "Sweet Georgia Brown" with an enthusiasm that suggested she, too, wanted to see Cuba win. The Cubs ran out onto the floor to a thunder of applause. Only one small section of the stadium was blanketed in red, signifying Manual supporters—the rest of the entire place was a sea of waving green and gold balloons, pennants, flags, posters, crepe-paper streamers,

caps, and scarves. The sellout crowd was stamping its feet, screaming, "Let's go, Cuba! Let's go! Let's go all the way!" The newspapers
reported the next day, "Never in the history of this thirty-five-year-
old classic was there a more popular team in Kentucky than Coach
Jack Story's Cubs."

In preparing his team to meet Manual for the third time,
Coach Story had changed his defensive strategy. In those two earlier
games, when Manual had beaten them, the Cubs had played their
routine man-to-man defense. For this competition, Coach Story
switched guard duty, as he had done successfully in the game they
won against Corbin. He had Howie guard Phil Grawmeyer, Manual's big All-State center, six inches taller than Howie. He told Doodle
to guard Curtis Moffett, Manual's six-foot-three All-State forward.
Although all of Manual's players, including substitutes, were excellent, these two boys were exceptionally high scorers. Grawmeyer
alone had made 29 points in the last game Cuba had played against
Manual. Coach Story was determined not to let him outplay his
team again. In instructing Howie, he repeated that quaint expression he'd used when he had told him to guard Corbin's Jerry Bird:
"Howie, you run around him like a guinea chasing corn." Coach
Story was confident his boys could stop Grawmeyer from making
as many baskets as the big center was capable of making. He told
Doodle, "If the Manual players try to lob the ball toward the backboard so that Grawmeyer can get the ball over Howie, you sag back
and slap the ball away. Howie, do not let Grawmeyer get that ball."

As the Cubs entered the gymnasium from their locker room,
they looked around the Coliseum. They knew that this time they
could fulfill their dream. Yet, as the game began, it looked like last
year's disappointment all over again, even though they had changed
their defensive strategy. Immediately, Grawmeyer and Moffett
moved their team out to leads of 6-1 and then 9-3 in the first four
minutes. Howie made a jump shot and Jimmie Webb a free throw to

trim the Manual edge to 13-9. But then Moffett made his free throw and Duffy Franklin a long set shot, putting Manual ahead 16-9 at the end of the first quarter. Suffering the stress of knowing that this was their *only* chance at winning the championship, the Cubs were so jittery they hit only three of eighteen shots.

At the beginning of the second quarter, Doodle made a foul shot. Moffett tipped in a basket and Malcolm Roessler hit a driving shot, doubling Manual's lead to 20-10. The Cubs fought back but still trailed at halftime, 30-24.

During the halftime break in the locker room, the Cubs circled penitently around Coach Story, listening to his new strategy. He moved Doodle to the side and put Pollock on the pivot, telling Pollock to draw Grawmeyer out to allow Doodle to drive under. Howie was still to guard Grawmeyer.

Without changing the pitch of his voice a shade, he reminded them that this was the last time they would ever all play basketball together—after five years, this was the last time. Then he pulled a telegram from his inside coat pocket, saying it had been handed to him just before the game started. It was from Jimmy Jones, who had been a starter and the captain of their team in the 1951 championship games. He had graduated the previous year and was in the navy. Coach Story read the message, which simply said, "Hey, boys, win this one for me!" Doodle blurted out, "Let's do it! I'll be damned if we're going to let Manual beat us! Let's go!"

When the Cubs came out for the second-half warm-ups to the peppy beat of their theme song, the arena erupted in their support. It was as if the crowd sensed what Cuba's last-ditch effort would be. A member of the Clark County team that had beaten the Cubs for the championship the year before, Louis Snowden, later said, "I never saw anything like that game before or since. When Cuba came out onto the floor at the half, everybody except the Manual fans stood up and yelled for them. I remember looking around the Coliseum,

Doodle is joined by Mary Belle Shelby, one of Cuba's thousands of supporters, outside the Phoenix Hotel in Lexington on the morning after the Cubs' triumph. (Photo courtesy of Charles Floyd.)

and I saw across the court only one little patch of red sitting in the section for the Manual fans. Everybody else in the whole place was waving green and gold and screaming for Cuba to win."

Howie, Doodle, Jimmie, Joe Buddy, and Bill Pollock, who had replaced Raymon, bounded out in the second half with a spirit that only a five-year-old dream could inspire. Like some rudely awakened giant, they started the come-from-behind drive their fans were hoping for. Bill Pollock began the scoring by getting his first points in the tournament on a pass from Howie to pull the margin to 4 points. Grawmeyer followed by hitting one of two foul shots. Joe Buddy made a basket on a pass from Doodle. Then Doodle stole the ball from Moffett and scored. Cuba was now behind only 31-30. The teams exchanged baskets and foul shots on a fairly even basis, with Manual staying in front until Joe Buddy scored on a pass from Howie, putting the Cubs ahead for the first time: 41-40. Although Grawmeyer scored one basket before the third quarter ended, Howie

Presentation of the 1952 championship trophy to the Cuba team. (Photo courtesy of Donald Poyner.)

and Doodle each contributed a basket and Joe Buddy a free throw to end the quarter with Cuba ahead 46-42.

The last quarter started with a tip-in by Grawmeyer for Manual. Doodle then rebounded his own shot, and Bill Pollock made a basket the same way. Grawmeyer hit a shot over Doodle's head, making the score 50-46. At that point, Cuba went into a stall that many thought was alone worth the price of admission. The rules at that time favored a great ball-handling team like Cuba. For four of the last six minutes, Cuba kept the ball, declining to shoot nine free throws, and brought the ball in from the side court instead. With only a minute left in the game, three of Manual's starters—Gaslin, Roessler, and Moffett—fouled out of the game as they desperately tried to get the ball from Howie.

With two minutes and forty-five seconds left, Jimmie Webb dashed to the hoop and made a basket. Now it was 52-46, with Cuba ahead. Still, there was a long way to go, with plenty of time

Coach Story and Howie Crittenden didn't seem to mind the chilly ride in a convertible as they showed off the 1952 championship trophy during the ride in the motorcade from Eggner's Ferry to Mayfield for a celebration. (Photo courtesy of Howard Crittenden.)

for the Crimsons to come back, which they started to do when little Neal Skeeters cut Cuba's lead to 52-48. Moffett followed with a tip-in before Doodle answered for Cuba with a lay-in. Then Moffett streaked in for an easy hoop, cutting Cuba's lead to 54-52. Only one minute and three seconds were left.

In a grandstand performance, Doodle made another bucket with fifty-two seconds left, putting Cuba ahead, 56-52, and Manual unable to score when it had the ball. There were only forty seconds left to play. For those last seconds, the crowd, except for Manual fans, was screaming as loudly as it could in unison with the Cuba cheerleaders, *Hey! Hey! Whaddaya say! Let's go, Cuba! All the way!* Cuba went back into its stall and passed the ball to—who else?—Howie.

The waning moments were sweet. While Manual went after Howie with increasing desperation, he retreated down long paths of trial and experience. He led Manual across worn patches of country clay and creaky country gym floors. He led it down miles of dusty country roads and through all those winter days and summer nights of practice at home in Graves County. He led Manual farther than it could follow. In the last eighteen seconds, Jimmie Webb, a reliable workhorse during the entire tournament, sneaked in for a basket, making the final score Cuba 58, Manual 52.

Cuba's dream season was complete.

Epilogue

In the heart of the Jackson Purchase
'neath the sun's warm glow
Lies the home of dear old Cuba,
sweetest name I know.
May we cherish our traditions,
wave the banner high,
May our love for dear old Cuba
live and never die.
                    —Cuba School alma mater

At the closing ceremony of the 1952 state tournament, Howie and Doodle, for the second straight year, were among the ten boys chosen for the All-State Tournament Team. Linville Puckett from Clark County was selected for the third straight year. The other Kentucky greats were Phil Grawmeyer from Manual and his teammates Curtis Moffett and Neal Skeeters. Also named were Garnard Martin from Hindman, Jerry Bird from Corbin, and Carlos Irwin of Breckenridge County.

The Cubs' trip home was a triumphant procession. As they moved through the state, word of their coming spread ahead of them. People in towns and tiny communities along the route packed the streets to wave flags and to cheer for them. At Horse Cave in central Kentucky, the local hotel owner treated them to steak dinners. In Trigg County, 750 fans met them, and at Eggner's Ferry Bridge the welcoming crowd was estimated at 4,000. The motorcade from Eggner's Ferry Bridge to Mayfield stretched for fourteen miles. Newspapers estimated that 12,000 people stood patiently in the cold weather to greet the team in the courthouse square. When the Cubs finally arrived in the square, the cheering lasted more than fifteen minutes. Again there was a round of speech making. Coach Story said simply, "I'm mighty glad we could bring back the trophy." Then each player said a few words. When his turn came, Howie could not hold back tears. In a trembling voice he said, "There are two things I am proud of today. First, we won the tournament, and second, Mr. Story said we made him feel like a young mule." Everyone laughed, knowing that was such an uncharacteristic expression for Story.

The following week the Cubs toured the Jackson Purchase, showing off their championship trophy. The purpose behind the tour was to inspire other high schools teams to set goals and to work hard at achieving them. The slogan in the region was "Let's build our teams next season, so we can keep the trophy west of the Tennessee River!"

Jack Story

Coach Story received many honors for leading the Cuba Cubs to victory. He was named head coach for the West Kentucky team in the first annual East-West game, played as part of the University of Kentucky athletic clinic in August 1952, and he was selected to head a group of high school all-stars in games across the state. After the Cubs graduated from high school and left for college, Jack Story left the Cuba School too to become head basketball coach at Mayfield High School. He took Mayfield to the state tournament three times, in 1955, 1956, and 1962, but never again brought home the championship. Jack Story became known as the dean of western Kentucky high school basketball. He won 478 games in his coaching career, and he never had a losing season.

In the early 1960s, he began having serious problems with his balance and speech. A series of tests showed that he had an inoperable malignant brain tumor. When his illness forced him to retire from coaching in the fall of 1965, he reflected, "I guess I have realized about everything a high school coach could want in basketball."

Jack Story faced his greatest challenge with courage and dignity. He died on the morning of September 8, 1971, at Baptist Memorial Hospital in Memphis, Tennessee. He was only fifty-four years old. With him were those he loved best: his wife, Mary Lee, his daughters, Carolyn and Barbara, and his son, Rex. He was buried in Highland Park Cemetery in Mayfield. One of the pallbearers at his funeral was Howie Crittenden. Mary Lee, who never remarried, died in August 1998 and is buried near his grave.

After Graduation

Both Doodle and Howie were selected to play in the North-South Game, an honor accorded to twenty-four of the best high school players in the United States. From these twenty-four players, five, including Howie, were selected as High School All-Americans by Chuck Taylor, executive director of the Converse Basketball Shoe Company. Howie and Doodle also played for the All-State Team.

Coach Diddle came to Pilot Oak to visit Howie and Doodle and their parents in their homes. He invited the boys to play basketball for him at Western Kentucky University in Bowling Green, but he failed to persuade either one of them to do so. Both boys had received many offers from other colleges, but they had no guidance from anyone on how to choose among the offers. Some politicians offered Howie a full scholarship to Murray State, promising, along with many other perks, to give his dad a job with the highway department. Knowing how much it would help his parents if his dad had a steady job with a good salary and benefits, Howie agreed to attend Murray.

Doodle also accepted the scholarship Murray offered him. Joe Buddy, Donald Poyner, and Bobby McClain enrolled there as well. Jimmie Webb worked for nearly a year before he too enrolled at Murray, in the fall of 1953. All but Doodle graduated from the institution with bachelor's and master's degrees in education and went on to successful careers in education—as coaches, teachers, principals, and administrators.

Doodle Floyd

Charles "Doodle" Floyd transferred to Northeast Mississippi Junior College in Booneville, Mississippi. Here, in 1954, he led the nation in scoring, with an average of 38 points a game. From there he went to Mississippi Southern (now Southern Mississippi) and played basketball for a year. He became disabled after he suffered a serious back injury, and had to withdraw from school. While still recuperating from surgery, he applied for an emergency temporary teaching certificate, which at that time allowed one to teach without a degree. He taught history and physical education at Farmington High School in Graves County for a year. Then he accepted an offer to play for Mississippi College in Clinton, Mississippi. But after a year his back problems again caused him to withdraw. He went to work for Reynolds Aluminum in Phoenix, Arizona, playing on the Reynolds basketball team in an American Amateur Union basketball league. But his back problems prevented him from playing basketball the way he once had, so he gave up playing entirely and moved to Knoxville, Tennessee, where he married Mary Lou Martin and opened a successful industrialized painting business, which he operated until his retirement in 1998. He and Mary had two sons. Sadly, she lost her battle with cancer on July 3, 2013. In good physical condition, Doodle swims nearly every morning and regularly plays basketball with friends in a nearby gym. He has also discovered the joy of books and has become an avid reader. He keeps in close touch with his childhood friends and others in Graves County and visits them once a year. He also communicates regularly with his good friend Phil Rollins, who was once his opponent, an All-American center from Wickliffe. Doodle was inducted into the Kentucky High School Athletic Association Hall of Fame on April 12, 2008.

Howie Crittenden

Howard "Howie" Crittenden went on to have an outstanding career at Murray State University both athletically and academically. He held the all-time Murray State scoring record in basketball for thirty-three years, from 1956 to 1989. He has been awarded many honors since receiving his master's degree. In 1970 he was elected a member of the Murray State University Athletic Hall of Fame, and for three years at Murray he was voted a member of the All-Ohio Valley Conference.

After college Howie was drafted by the New York Knicks. However, he chose to play in the AAU National Industrial Basketball League for the Peoria Caterpillars, and he was selected as an AAU All-American in Basketball in 1957, 1958, and 1960. In 1958 Howie was chosen for the first U.S. basketball team to ever compete against the Soviet Union. This team toured the Soviet Union for a month, winning all six games against the Russians.

On March 14, 1989, Howard was inducted into the Kentucky High School Athletic Association Hall of Fame, along with Gay Brewer, a former Masters champion; Wes Unseld, NBA great; Frank

Ramsey, ex–Boston Celtic star, and others. In 2004 he was inducted into the prestigious Kentucky Athletic Hall of Fame, and on July 20, 2013, he was inducted into the Kentucky High School Basketball Hall of Fame.

After teaching in several high schools in western Kentucky, Howard became principal of Calloway County High School in Murray, Kentucky. He was there from 1966 to 1974 and then moved to Henderson, Kentucky, where he was principal of one of the largest schools in the state—Henderson County Senior High School. In 1983 he was recognized by the *Louisville Courier-Journal* as a model high school principal. In 1990 Howard was honored as Kentucky Secondary Principal of the Year.

After retiring in 1995, he moved to Bowling Green, Kentucky, where he worked as a substitute principal for a few years before retiring a second time. At present, he and his wife, Meg, live in Murray. He has one son by his first marriage.

Jimmie Webb

Jimmie Webb and Martha Casey married at the beginning of their senior year in high school, September 1951, and they lived with his parents until that summer. After graduation both got jobs and moved into an apartment in Mayfield. In 1953, the same year their first child, Terri, was born, Jimmie enrolled in Murray but would often have to stay out a semester to work. After their second child, Jeff, was born in 1957, Jimmie received a temporary teaching certificate and went to work teaching in schools in Wingo and then in Clinton, Kentucky. After Martha got a job as a legal secretary in Mayfield and the couple hired a babysitter, Jimmie was able to return to Murray. He earned his bachelor's degree in 1961. Shortly after that, he and Martha moved to Effingham, Illinois, where he was hired to teach. Martha found good work as an assistant to an accountant. During the twelve years they lived in Effingham, Jimmie continued to work on his master's degree, which he received in 1968. He was principal of a junior high school in Teutopolis, Illinois, a role he held for twenty years. He retired in 1992 and became an adjunct professor at the community college in Teutopolis.

He and Martha, forever sweethearts, enjoyed traveling and were looking forward to more good years together. While they were planning a trip abroad, she became ill and died unexpectedly on January 12, 2011.

Donald Poyner

Shortly after Donald Poyner received his master's degree from Murray State University, he was hired as the assistant superintendent of Graves County Schools. He was the director of personnel and curriculum. He retired from full-time employment in 1999, and since then has been working part-time as an administrative assistant.

While he was working full-time, Donald organized and managed a men's semipro softball team that competed in the American Softball Association. His team played 110 games a year over a five-year period, and it holds the national record for winning five straight regional championships. Donald and his wife, Dortha, live in Mayfield and have two daughters.

Bill Pollock

Bill Pollock was the boy whom Coach Story recruited from Fancy Farm and who turned out to be a valuable reserve during his senior year at Cuba. After high school graduation, Bill joined the navy for a stint, after which he worked in Michigan for a while. Then he moved back to Mayfield, married, and went to work in the sheriff's office. After being chief deputy for four years, he left to work for the municipal gas department. In 1981 he opened his own plumbing business, which he operated until recently. Although retired, he now works part-time for the sheriff's department as a deputy. He and his wife have three children.

Classmates

The Cubs team manager Bobby McClain is a retired school administrator and lives on his farm outside Cuba. Raymon McClure died young in a farming accident. Robert Peters, who broke the tension on the bus that was taking the Manual team and the Cubs to the last tournament game, died in his early thirties of a brain tumor. Jimmy Jones, the only senior on the team in 1951, is deceased, as are the two reserves: Paul Simpson and Harold Roberts. Paul died in an automobile accident in the early 1980s. Harold Roberts, Ted Bradley, and his good friend Joe Buddy Warren all died of cancer. Ted was a truck driver for most of his life with an outstanding record for safety. Joe Buddy graduated from Murray and coached for many years at Benton, Kentucky. Then he went into the real estate business in Benton for a while. After the schools were consolidated and Graves County High School was established, Joe Buddy went back to coaching at the new high school.

Cheerleaders Carolyn Work and Barbara Harper are deceased. Howie's twin, Helen, also a cheerleader, was killed in an automobile accident just outside of Mayfield one summer afternoon in 1996.

Dr. Marion Page

Until the consolidation of the schools in the 1940s, Dr. Marion Page, the physician for southern Graves County, was one of the trustees of the Cuba School. Born and reared in the Cuba area, Dr. Page knew the isolation that people in the Purchase experienced and wanted to give the children opportunities that exposed them to the outside world. He insisted that the faculty come from places other than Graves County or the Jackson Purchase if at all possible. He wanted not only his own four children but all the children in Cuba to be exposed to ideas, beliefs, and cultures other than their own. While he was trustee, he provided room and board in his own home for the single teachers when they arrived. He believed that the more his own children were in the company of educated people, on a personal as well as an academic level, the more likely they were to grow intellectually and to learn to be tolerant of different views. During the evening meal in the doctor's home, the teachers and family shared interesting conversations—but they seldom discussed sports.

Next to his neat, white-framed home, Dr. Page's little office is still standing—silent and dusty. The day I visited it, dried leaves had blown in and were scattered about on the floor. His black leather examining table is there, and the waiting room's straight-backed oak chairs still line the walls. His large black records books, with patients' names and receipts written in his strong, clear handwriting, are strewn on top of the table in the back room he used as his office and pharmacy. Even some of the little white pill envelopes he used to blow into to open still lie on the shelf. His daughters are both now deceased: Hattie Page Glenn passed away on January 16, 2005, and Beth Page Belote passed away on October 8, 2012.

Cuba, Kentucky

The little community no longer looks the way it did when the Cubs lived there. Cuba is neither lively nor thriving anymore. The large oak trees that once lined the main road and shaded the homes are gone. In some places you may see an old trailer, a dilapidated car, or a pickup truck in various stages of disrepair. What were once well-kept lawns are mostly weeds, and maybe a few pieces of old rusted farm machinery. Where lilacs and rose bushes grew in abundance are discarded fast-food bags and empty drink cans.

Nearly all of the barns are gone, and some of the dirt roads that the boys ran up and down, tossing and dribbling basketballs, are overgrown with wild bushes and weeds. The few people who live in the Cuba area no longer all know each other by first name. In the evenings they do not sit on their front porches and talk as the folks once did. Their doors are closed, shades pulled down, and their televisions are on.

Gone also are the two general stores where the village folk used to congregate, where the old store setters teased kids and played checkers every day, where folks gathered to listen to the radio broadcasting the news, ball games, or Grand Ole Opry. The old Wagoner's store in Pilot Oak has been torn down, too, although the present Pilot Oak store looks something like it did when Doodle and Howie lived there.

Off in the grassy fields remain a few cisterns and neglected old smokehouses with rusty, netless basketball goals nailed to the side walls—all silent reminders of days long gone. Noticeably missing from the landscape are little boys chasing each other or playing basketball.

The little Cuba schoolhouse where the Cubs' dream was born has long since been torn down, and with it went all its furnishings, including the study hall table on which Jimmie Webb in 1948 carved the words "Cuba Cubs—State Champions, 1952." The old school was replaced with a modern building for grades K through 6. It has a modern curriculum and is staffed with certified faculty and administrators. However, since the Cubs graduated, nothing quite as remarkable as their achievement has happened.

In the last half century or more, small rural schools across the United States have all but disappeared. They have been swallowed up—consolidated into larger ones, despite some objections. Whether or not consolidation has improved American education is debatable.

The Cuba Cubs, 1951–1952 Kentucky State High School Basketball champions. Front row, seated on floor: managers Robert Peters, Rex Story, and Bobby McClain. Second row: Paul Simpson, Jimmy Brown, Joe Buddy Warren, Howie Crittenden, Jimmie Sims, and Ted Bradley. Top row: Coach Jack Story, Raymon McClure, Bill Pollock, Doodle Floyd, Harold Roberts, Drennon Bagwell, Jimmie Webb, and assistant coach Joe McPherson. (Cuba School yearbook photo.)

With their schools gone, little rural communities—like Cuba—have lost their sense of identity and purpose. If they exist at all now, they are as fragmented as cities. It is not likely that little Cuba's story will ever be repeated. And that magical kind of euphoria that the Cuba Cubs created—that euphoria that did not vanish quickly after the tournaments as sports' highs do today—also has disappeared from the American scene.

With their wise coach and loving support from the community, the spirited Cuba Cubs showed us that dreams do come true. The Cubs proved that no matter how poor and disadvantaged we may be, with imagination, determination, and hard work, we can set goals and achieve them. Cuba's story is the American dream.

Acknowledgments

This book is about real people and real events, and I could not have written it without the cooperation of those I wrote about. With kindness and patience, these people shared their memories, time, and resources. I am indebted to each of them.

I owe thanks also to many others who took time and trouble to help me along the way. Two good friends of mine for many years, Lucinda Evans and Jeffrey Douglas, deserve my special gratitude. A retired English teacher and book lover whose opinions I value, Cindy read the manuscript in its early form more than once and pointed to places that needed attention. A former colleague who is now the director of the library at Knox College in Galesburg, Illinois, Jeff is the person I have always turned to for advice about research and writing. He has often shown me different ways to think about a subject. He, too, read portions of the manuscript and offered insightful advice.

My brother-in-law James Walker scanned all the photographs. Donald Poyner, the first person (after Howie and Doodle) that I spoke with when I considered writing this book, has never failed to answer my numerous questions promptly and thoroughly. Donald helped me start my research by sending me the names and addresses of all the people associated with the Cuba Cubs in the 1940s and early 1950s.

I am grateful for the friendship and support of Coach Joe B. Hall, the award-winning gentleman basketball coach from the University of Kentucky, and his radio program manager, Jim Lankster. Serendipity and the Cuba Cubs brought us all together in early 2012. I appreciate the opportunities Coach Hall has given me to be on his and Coach Denny Crum's radio program and the attention he has given to this book.

I am indebted to Stacy Cain, expert legal secretary, who did the index; Nathan Lynn, in charge of the special collections section at the McCracken County Public Library in Paducah, Kentucky, found several of the old newspaper articles and photos featured in this book. Trish Corino, my daughter who lives nearby, did some typing for me; Amy Jones, my youngest daughter, who lives in Beattyville, Kentucky, read the manuscript and offered good advice; Scott Bailey, who is the husband of my oldest daughter, Beth, has on more than one occasion solved my computer problems. All of these young people were so pleasant in assisting me; they made chores that were tedious much less so.

Because of Ashley Runyon, editor at the University Press of Kentucky, I knew my manuscript was in good and caring hands. My special thanks go to the good-natured, sharp-eyed Robin DuBlanc, copyeditor, and Iris Law, editorial supervisor. And I appreciate Mack McCormick, publicist; Blair Thomas, who developed the web site for the online guide; and all the others at the press who participated in bringing this book to fruition. Any errors it may contain are mine alone.

Last, my deepest appreciation goes to Ulvester, my husband, to whom this book is dedicated. In dozens of ways, he helped me, as he always has no matter what the endeavor, every step of the way.

Bibliography

Books

Harrison, Lowell, and James C. Klotter. *A New History of Kentucky.* Lexington: University Press of Kentucky, 1997.

Klebber, John E., ed. *The Kentucky Encyclopedia.* Lexington: University Press of Kentucky, 1992.

Miller, Don. *The Carr Creek Legacy.* New York: Vantage, 1995.

Rice, Russell. *The Wildcat Legacy.* Virginia Beach, VA: JCP, 1982.

Stout, Louis. *Shadows of the Past: A History of the Kentucky High School Athletic League.* Lexington: Host Communications, 2006.

Newspaper Articles

Adair, Bob. "Colorful Cubs from Cuba Capture State Cage Crown with Cinderella Finish." *Lexington Herald-Leader,* March 23, 1952.

———. "Cuba Cubs Are Gone, but Won't Be Forgotten." *Lexington Herald-Leader,* March 24, 1952.

———. "Cubs Oust Hindman in 'Greatest' Semis." *Lexington Herald-Leader,* March 23, 1952.

———. "Cubs Win by 61-47 over Local Quintet; Hindman Routs MMI." *Lexington Herald-Leader,* March 22, 1952.

———. "Tourney Talk." *Lexington Herald-Leader,* March 24, 1952.

"Almost 2,000 Cage Fans to See Cuba-Selmer Game Here Tonight." *Mayfield Messenger,* January 21, 1952.

Anderson, Jack. "Clark County Opens Defense of State Title Today; Cuba Meets Corbin at 7:30." *Mayfield Messenger,* March 20, 1952.

————. "Crowd of 6,000, Eight-Mile Long Motorcade Turn out to Greet Runner-up Cuba Cubs Here Sunday." *Mayfield Messenger,* March 19, 1951.

————. "Cuba Meets Symsonia Tonight in Regional Semi-finals; Wickliffe Plays Bardwell." *Mayfield Messenger,* March 13, 1952.

————."Cuba Still Popular." *Mayfield Messenger,* March 21, 1952.

————. "Doodle Floyd Sparks Cubs to Fourth Period Win over Corbin, Henry Clay Is Next." *Mayfield Messenger,* March 21, 1952.

————. "Sports before Your Eyes." *Mayfield Messenger,* March 10, 1951.

————. "Sports before Your Eyes." *Mayfield Messenger,* January 21, 1952.

————. "Sports before Your Eyes." *Mayfield Messenger,* March 4, 1952.

Anderson, Jess G. "Among Other Things." *Mayfield Messenger,* March 18, 1951.

Atkins, Jerry. "Jack Story Legend Will Live Years after His Death." *Paducah Sun-Democrat,* September 10, 1972.

Carrico, Johnny. "Clark County Rips Cuba 69-44 to Win Crown." *Louisville Courier-Journal,* March 17, 1951.

————. "Cuba Conquers Manual for State Title 58-52." *Louisville Courier-Journal,* March 22, 1952.

————. "Hoopin It Up." *Louisville Courier-Journal,* March 25, 1952.

Carter, Bill. "The Colorful Cubs." *Paducah Sun-Democrat,* March 10, 1957.

————. "Contests Undecided until Final Minutes." *Paducah Sun-Democrat,* December 29, 1951.

————. "Tourney Teams Have Good Marks." *Paducah Sun-Democrat,* March 11, 1952.

"Clark County Defeats Cuba Cubs 57 to 48." *Mayfield Messenger,* February 12, 1952.

"Clark County Touted as the Team to Beat." *Mayfield Messenger,* March 18, 1952.

"Confident Cuba Five Leaves for Lexington; State Meet Opens with 2 Games Tonight." *Mayfield Messenger,* March 19, 1952.

"Cuba Beats Warren County 64-38 in Tourney Warmup." *Mayfield Messenger,* January 24, 1952.

"Cuba Blasts Selmer Quintet 69-50 in Charity Contest." *Mayfield Messenger,* January 22, 1952.

"Cuba Bows to Manual Crimsons in Finals of Louisville Tourney." *Mayfield Messenger,* January 28, 1952.

"Cuba Clashes with Clark Co. Quintet Tonight." *Mayfield Messenger,* February 11, 1952.

"Cuba Clashes with Wickliffe Tonight at 8 P.M. in Finals of First Region Tournament." *Mayfield Messenger,* March 14, 1952.

"Cuba Cubs Blast Lowes Blue Devils by 116 to 49 Score." *Mayfield Messenger,* January 8, 1952.

"Cuba Cubs Blast Rollins-less Wickliffe Blue Tigers 68-33." *Mayfield Messenger,* February 7, 1952.

"Cuba Cubs Close Season with Win over Lone Oak." *Mayfield Messenger,* February 16, 1952.

"Cuba Cubs Defeat Caverna Quintet by Score of 36-31." *Mayfield Messenger,* January 19, 1952.

"Cuba Cubs Defeat Symsonia 58-42; Farmington Beaten by Sedalia." *Mayfield Messenger,* January 23, 1952.

"Cuba Cubs First Quintet to Represent Graves County Twice in State Tournament." *Mayfield Messenger,* March 16, 1952.

"Cuba Cubs Slight Favorite to Win Paducah Christmas Invitational." *Mayfield Messenger,* December 27, 1951.

"Cuba Cubs Solid Favorites to Cop Third District Cage Meet." *Mayfield Messenger,* March 3, 1952.

"Cuba Cubs to Meet Best Teams in Two States within Next Eight Days." *Mayfield Messenger,* January 17, 1952.

"Cuba Cubs Win Cage Tourney at Maysville." *Mayfield Messenger,* November 26, 1951.

"Cuba Cubs Win 18th by Defeating Sedalia Lions 59-41." *Mayfield Messenger,* January 16, 1952.

"Cuba Defeats Male 63 to 50; Meet Campbellsville at 1:15 P.M. today." *Mayfield Messenger,* January 25, 1952.

"Cuba 86, Crittenden 48." *Mayfield Messenger,* December 28, 1951.

"Cuba-Lone Oak Game Tonight Is Sellout." *Mayfield Messenger,* February 16, 1952.

"Cuba Mauls Lone Oak 72-54 to Win Paducah Christmas Cage Tourney." *Mayfield Messenger,* December 30, 1951.

"Cuba Meets Bandana, Lone Oak vs. Sharpe in Paducah JCC Tourney." *Mayfield Messenger,* December 29, 1951.

"Cuba, Minus 3 Regulars, Defeated by Allen County 49-48; Wingo Wins." *Mayfield Messenger,* February 4, 1952.

"Cuba Not Going to State Meet 'Just for the Ride'; Big Sendoff Planned for Cubs." *Mayfield Messenger,* March 13, 1951.

"Cuba Outlasts Hindman 44-42." *Mayfield Messenger,* March 22, 1952.

"Cuba Pull out 64-41 Victory over St. Mary's." *Mayfield Messenger,* December 3 1951.

"Cuba-Selmer Game Here Monday Night Complete Sellout." *Mayfield Messenger,* January 18, 1952.

"Cuba's First Region Champs Meet Covington Holmes in Lexington Thursday Night." *Mayfield Messenger,* March 11, 1951.

"Cuba Swamps Lowes High by 116-49." *Mayfield Messenger,* January 8, 1952.

"Cuba Swats Symsonia 86-56." *Mayfield Messenger,* December 18, 1951.

"Cuba to Visit 20 Towns in Area Tomorrow." *Mayfield Messenger,* March 24, 1952.

"Cuba Trounces Wickliffe in Invalids' Battle." *Mayfield Messenger,* February 6, 1952.

"Cuba, Wickliffe Clash at Murray Thursday." *Mayfield Messenger,* January 8, 1952.

"Cuba, Wickliffe Draw in Opposite Brackets in Regional Tourney; Cubs Beat Symsonia in District." *Mayfield Messenger,* March 10, 1952.

"Cuba Wins Regional Tourney; Defeats Wickliffe 54-42." *Mayfield Messenger,* March 15, 1952.

"Cubs Leave for State Meet at Lexington; Mass Exodus of Inhabitants to Follow." *Mayfield Messenger,* March 14, 1951.

"Favored Manual Defeated in Finals; Cubs First Graves Team to Win Championship." *Mayfield Messenger,* March 22, 1952.

Finch, Jerry. "All Tournament Selections Dominated by Winning Cuba and Runner-up Reds." *Lexington Herald-Leader,* March 23, 1952.

———. "Hindman One to Watch in '53 Meets: Fourth-Down, One-to-Go Plays Critical." *Lexington Herald-Leader,* March 24, 1952.

"Former Coach Jack Story Is Honored Here." *Mayfield Messenger,* n.d.

Hall, F. M. "Cuba School Closing Revives Memories of '52 State Title." *Paducah Sun-Democrat,* March 20, 1977.

"It's Cuba vs Hindman and Manual vs Clark County in Semi-finals." *Lexington Herald-Leader,* March 22, 1952.

"The Jackson Purchase Historical Society Sesquicentennial Edition." *Mayfield Messenger,* December 27, 1969.

Kellow, Edd. "The Big Enigma." *Paducah Sun-Democrat,* March 17, 1951.

———. "Cuba Conquers Stubborn Henry Clay 61-47 to Reach Semi-finals." *Paducah Sun-Democrat,* March 21, 1952.

———. "Cuba Defeated 69-44 by Clark County Cardinals in Finals of State Tournament." *Paducah Sun-Democrat,* March 18, 1951.

———. "Cuba Downs Wickliffe 54-42." *Paducah Sun-Democrat,* March 15, 1952.

———. "Cuba, Manual Score Close Victories to Reach Finals." *Paducah Sun-Democrat,* March 22, 1952.

———. "Cuba Overcomes Wickliffe in Great Contest." *Paducah Sun-Democrat,* March 10, 1951.

———. "Cuba Plays University Tonight After 38-37 Win over Holmes in Opener." *Paducah Sun-Democrat,* March 16, 1951.

———. "Cuba Residents Prepare to Follow Cubs." *Paducah Sun-Democrat,* March 13, 1951.

———. "Cuba Sparkles in Win over Demons." *Paducah Sun-Democrat,* March 22, 1952.

———. "Cuba Tops Whitesburg 65-52 to Play Clark for Crown." *Paducah Sun-Democrat,* March 17, 1951.

———. "Cuba Tours Jackson Purchase, Showing Championship Trophy." *Paducah Sun-Democrat,* March 25, 1952.

———. "Cuba Went After Bacon, Ended up with Gold." *Paducah Sun-Democrat,* March 24, 1952.

———. "Floyd, Bird Each Hit 22 in Battle of Centers." *Paducah Sun-Democrat,* March 20, 1952.

———. "Floyd, Crittenden Hand Flash First Loss." *Paducah Sun-Democrat,* December 28, 1951.

———. "Floyd, Crittenden Team Up to Hand Flash First Loss." *Paducah Sun-Democrat,* December 30, 1951.

———. "Late Cuba Rally Drops University." *Paducah Sun-Democrat,* March 17, 1951.

———. "Time Out—Few Will Return." *Paducah Sun-Democrat,* March 22, 1952.

———. "Tournament Talk." *Paducah Sun-Democrat,* March 16, 1951.

"Legendary Cuba Graduates Reunited After 25 Years." *Mayfield Messenger,* n.d., 1977.

Malony, Mark. "The Sweet Sixteen—Magic Moments." *Lexington Herald-Leader,* March 4, 1979.

"Manual Beats Cuba Cubs 48-41; Floyd Injured." *Mayfield Messenger,* January 18, 1952.

"Pair of High Scoring Quintets to Meet in Charity Game Here Monday." *Mayfield Messenger,* January 18, 1952.

Pepper, Don. "Blue Tigers Top Bardwell in Last Half Surge by 74-62; Cubs Defeat Symsonia 61-34." *Paducah Sun-Democrat,* March 14, 1952.

Powell, Bill. "Memories of Cuba's Big Day . . . 25 Years Haven't Dimmed a Legend." *Louisville Courier-Journal,* March n.d., 1977.

"Sedalia-Symsonia, Cuba-Wingo Clash in Semi-finals Tonight." *Mayfield Messenger,* March 7, 1952.

Shropshire, Larry. "Down in Front." *Lexington Herald-Leader,* March 19, 1952.

————. "Down in Front." *Lexington Herald-Leader,* March 21, 1952.

Smith, Mike. "Cuba's Colorful Clowns Laughed Last (and Best)." *Lexington Herald-Leader,* February 20, 1977.

"Sports—On the Eve of the 'Sweet 16.'" *Mayfield Messenger,* March n.d., 1977.

"Symsonia Edges Sedalia in Semi-finals, Meets Cuba Tonight for Championship." *Mayfield Messenger,* March 8, 1952.

"Symsonia vs. Brewers, Cuba Cubs vs. Clinton in Regional Tonight." *Mayfield Messenger,* March 12, 1952.

Turley, Mike. "State Champion Cuba Cub Cagers Gather for a 30th-Year Reunion." *Mayfield Messenger,* [?], 1982.

"2,000 Attend 'Open House' to Honor State Basketball Champs." *Mayfield Messenger,* March 25, 1952.

"Wickliffe Wins Murray Tourney after Defeating Cuba Cubs 52-51." *Mayfield Messenger,* January 11, 1952.

Interviews

Beth Belote, 1994.
Ted Bradley, 1997.
Jimmie Brown, 1997.
Lon Carter, 1997.

Howard Crittenden, 1989, 1995, 1997, 2010, 2011, 2012.
Rachel Davis, 1997.
Charles "Doodle" Floyd, 1989, 1997, 2010, 2011, 2012.
Hattie Glenn, 1994.
Pauline Harper, 1998.
Al McClain, 1998.
Bobby McClain, 1997.
Otis McPherson, 1997.
Bill Pollock, 1995.
Donald Poyner, 1997.
Lewis Snowden, 1998.
Story family, 1998.
Mrs. Rex Story, 1998.
Joe B. Warren, 1997.
Jimmy and Martha Webb, 1998, 2010, 2011, 2012.

Written Responses to Individual Questionnaires

Ted Bradley, 1994.
Helen Crittenden Glover, 1994.
Mason Harris, 1994.
William R. James, 1994.
Joe B. Warren, 1994.
Jimmie Webb, 1994.
Martha Webb, 1994.

Index